Redefining Mondays

Pathways to Work-Life Harmony

By
Leah DeMarest

Redefining Mondays

Pathways to Work-Life Harmony

Table of Contents

Introduction

Welcome to a journey that reimagines the potential of Mondays, transforming them from a day of dread to a pivotal moment that sets the tone for a productive week, balanced life, and improved job performance. The first day of the workweek does not have to be a source of anxiety or discontent; it can be an opportunity for growth, motivation, and joy. This introduction serves as the doorway into a world where Mondays become as beloved as Fridays, rooted in the belief that with the right mindset, tools, and habits, every part of the week can be fulfilling.

The phenomenon known as the "Monday Blues" is more than just a popular term; it's a reflection of the collective apprehension many feel as they transition from the freedom of the weekend to the structure of the workweek. However, it's crucial to understand that the discomfort of Mondays is not insurmountable. Instead, it's a signpost pointing towards areas of our lives and routines that could benefit from introspection and adjustment.

Imagine starting your week not with a sense of heaviness but with enthusiasm and a clear mind. This vision can become your reality. Through the following pages, we'll embark on a transformative path that focuses on maximizing the quality of your Mondays, thereby enhancing your overall work-life balance and performance. These enhancements are not just about the hours spent at work but about improving the quality of life itself.

The goal is clear: to equip you with knowledge, strategies, and actionable steps that address both the symptoms and root causes of the Monday slump. By adopting a holistic approach, we'll cover a myriad of strategies, from adjusting Sunday routines to reconfiguring the mental frameworks with which we approach our workweek. It's about empowering you with the resilience to face Mondays head-on and with a smile.

Think of this as not just a guide but a toolkit for invigorating your Mondays, with ripple effects that touch every aspect of your professional and personal lives. The transformation advocated here is gradual and deeply personal. It requires honesty, effort, and a commitment to self-improvement, but the rewards are substantial and far-reaching.

Our journey will debunk myths about productivity and happiness at work, challenge you to redefine your understanding of balance, and encourage you to find joy in every day of the week. This is a call to shift perspectives, to see Mondays as an opportunity for a fresh start and to approach them with a strategy that ensures they're as invigorating as they are productive.

By addressing the dread of Mondays at its core, we'll explore how to foster a mindset that thrives on challenges and views the start of the week as an opportunity for progress and positivity. This mindset shift is crucial for not just surviving but thriving in today's fast-paced world.

Understanding the root causes of the Monday Blues is just the beginning. From there, we'll delve into practical strategies for designing evenings and mornings that set you up for success. These strategies are about creating routines that energize and inspire, laying the groundwork for days that are productive, fulfilling, and balanced.

Much of our focus will be on cultivating habits and practices that improve not only your experience of Mondays but your entire week and, by extension, your life. It's about making small, sustainable changes that lead to significant improvements in how you feel about work and your ability to balance the various aspects of your life effectively.

In today's constantly connected world, it's easy to feel overwhelmed by the demands of work and personal life. This book offers a sanctuary, a place to step back and assess how you approach your week, with a particular focus on transforming the most challenging day into a cornerstone for success.

Moreover, we'll explore how employers can play a pivotal role in mitigating the Monday Blues, fostering a culture that supports a healthy work-life balance, and by doing so, increasing job satisfaction and performance across the board. While the primary audience of this book is employees, employers too can glean insights into creating a more positive, productive, and harmonious work environment.

Let's redefine what Mondays mean and turn them into a day you look forward to, not because the challenges are fewer, but because your capacity to handle them has grown. This book is an invitation to those who believe that the start of the week can bring joy, motivation, and productivity in equal measure.

By implementing the strategies discussed, you'll not only change how you face Mondays but also discover a profound sense of balance and achievement that permeates your work and personal life. The transition starts with understanding, shifts with action, and settles with a new way of living that embraces every day with enthusiasm and confidence.

As we move through this journey together, keep an open mind and heart. Be ready to challenge your preconceptions about work, life, and especially Mondays. The transformation you're about to embark on is both deep and encompassing, touching every aspect of your professional and personal life. It's time to turn the page on the Monday Blues and step into a world where Mondays are as welcome as a warm sunrise, signaling the start of another beautiful opportunity to live fully and work meaningfully.

Chapter 1:
Understanding the Monday Blues

As we turn the page from the introduction, we find ourselves face to face with a phenomenon so universal, yet often misunderstood—the Monday Blues. It's that familiar, heavy feeling that creeps in on Sunday evenings, casting a shadow over the remainder of our weekend. This chapter aims to peel back the layers of this experience, shedding light on its intricacies and origins. The Monday Blues isn't just a case of weekend withdrawal; it's a complex interplay of psychological and physical reactions to the abrupt transition from leisure back to structure.

Diving deeper, one can't ignore the role that our lifestyle choices on weekends play in exacerbating this angst. Excessive indulgence in food and drink, coupled with a shake-up in our sleep patterns, sets the stage for a less-than-ideal start to the week. Our bodies and minds are out of sync, and yet, we're expected to hit the ground running come Monday morning. It's not just about dreading the return to work; it's the tangible feeling of unwellness that many people report, backed by studies highlighting spikes in stress-related hormones and a notable dip in general health at the start of the week.

At its core, understanding the Monday Blues requires us to confront not just our weekend habits, but also our job satisfaction and mental health. Issues like burnout, anxiety, and a sense of misalignment with our work contribute significantly to this phenomenon. It's a sign, perhaps, that we're not just struggling with Monday; we're grappling with deeper discontentment. This chapter lays the groundwork for recognizing the Monday Blues not as an inevitable curse, but as a signal alerting us to areas of our lives that might be out of balance. With this understanding comes the power to transform our approach to Mondays, and indeed, our entire work-life balance.

What Are the Monday Blues?

Ever found yourself sprawled out on your bed, eyes glued to the ceiling, dreading the idea of peeling the covers back to face the world—especially when it's Monday? You're not alone; this feeling has a name: the Monday Blues. It's that tinge of melancholy, a cocktail of reluctance and mild dread, that seems to wash over us as we transition from the freedom and rest of the weekend back into the rigors of our workweek.

The Monday Blues can manifest in various ways: a sense of heaviness, a lack of motivation, irritability, or a profound desire to return to the bliss of the weekend. It's more than just a collective groan shared across social media; it's a palpable shift in our energy and enthusiasm for our tasks. It reflects our internal struggle with discipline and leisure, duty, and play. And while it might seem trivial to some, its impacts on our productivity, happiness, and work-life balance can be significant.

This sensation isn't born from laziness or a lack of professionalism. Instead, it's a natural response to abrupt transitions. Human beings are creatures of habit; we thrive on routine and predictability. The sudden change from the freedom of the weekend to the structure of a working Monday can be jarring. It's a reminder of the relentless pace of work-life, often leaving us longing for more personal time or dreading the potential stresses that lie in the week ahead.

Understanding the Monday Blues requires a gentle approach, one that acknowledges the legitimacy of these feelings while exploring their underpinnings. Are we dissatisfied with our jobs, or is it the idea of work itself that weighs heavily upon us? Perhaps it's the stark contrast between how we spend our weekends versus our weekdays that amplifies this dread. Investigating these feelings can illuminate deeper aspects of our relationship with work and rest.

Interestingly, the Monday Blues don't discriminate; they affect people across various professions, life stages, and backgrounds. It's a universal phenomenon that underscores a common human experience—the search for meaning and joy in what we do and the balance we strive to achieve between work and leisure.

Addressing the Monday Blues starts with recognizing its existence. It's not about dismissing these feelings as unwarranted or viewing them as obstacles to be bulldozed over. Instead, it's about listening to what these emotions are telling us about our wants, needs, and current life circumstances. This self-awareness is the first step toward reclaiming joy and productivity in our Mondays and, by extension, our entire lives.

It's also worth noting that the Monday Blues can be a signpost, pointing us towards aspects of our lives that may need adjustment or reconsideration. Perhaps it's the nature of our work, the balance we maintain between personal and professional life, or how we choose to recharge over the weekend. These feelings can serve as indicators, urging us to take inventory and adjust accordingly.

But how do we move beyond simply understanding the Monday Blues to actively mitigating their impact? It starts with small, intentional actions—tweaking our Sunday routines, adjusting how we perceive our work, and finding value in the tasks we undertake. The goal is not to eliminate the natural ebb and flow of our emotions throughout the week but to cultivate a more resilient and positive mindset as we face each Monday.

At the heart of the Monday Blues lies a powerful opportunity for growth and introspection. It challenges us to examine our perceptions of work, leisure, and the delicate balance between the two. It encourages us to reflect on our priorities, passions, and the alignment between our day-to-day activities and our broader life goals.

Embracing the complexity of the Monday Blues means understanding it's more than just a distaste for Mondays; it's a reflection of our relationship with work and its role in our lives. It invites us to consider how we can infuse more passion and purpose into our workweek, transforming our experience of Mondays from something we endure to something we look forward to—or at least, approach with a sense of calm and preparedness.

Ultimately, the Monday Blues serve as a reminder that our search for fulfillment and joy doesn't have to be limited to the weekend. By re-evaluating our routines, perspectives, and the meaning we derive from our work, we can challenge the notion that Mondays are inherently bleak. It's about shifting our mindset, finding value in our contributions, and recognizing the potential for growth and happiness in every day of the week, not just the ones that feel the freest.

To navigate the Monday Blues, we must first extend kindness to ourselves, allowing space for these feelings without judgment. Acknowledging and understanding our emotional responses is crucial. It paves the way for compassionate self-inquiry, helping us to identify practical steps to align our workweek with our values and desires. The task is not always easy, but the pursuit of a more balanced, gratifying professional life is undoubtedly worth the endeavor.

The Monday Blues can be a powerful catalyst for personal and professional transformation. By embracing and understanding these feelings, we can uncover the underlying causes and take actionable steps towards a more fulfilling work-life balance. Let Monday be a bridge, not a barrier, to a week filled with purpose, satisfaction, and joy.

Remember, every Monday offers a new beginning, a fresh start that holds the promise of possibility and growth. Let's shift our perspective, making the first day of the workweek a symbol of renewal and optimism. With the right mindset and strategies, we can overcome the Monday Blues, turning them from a source of dread to an opportunity for empowerment and positive change.

Why Do I Have the Monday Blues

Ever found yourself lying in bed on a Sunday evening, dreading the sound of your alarm going off the next morning? If yes, you're not alone in this struggle. As we peel back the layers to understand this phenomenon, it's crucial to recognize that the Monday Blues aren't just a catchy phrase but a reflection of our conflict with transition, expectations, and often dissatisfaction with our professional lives.

Let's start with the obvious yet often overlooked fact that humans are creatures of habit. Our bodies and minds thrive on routine, and the weekend provides us with a break from that routine. During these two days, we enjoy a significant degree of freedom from our work-related responsibilities. The stark contrast when Monday arrives is jarring. It's not just about returning to work; it's about re-entering a space that demands a different part of ourselves.

The transition from Sunday to Monday isn't solely about the physical act of going to work. It's emotionally taxing because it's also a transition from personal time that we control to a more structured time dictated by work responsibilities. This shift can feel particularly harsh if you're someone who craves autonomy over your time and tasks.

Moreover, the societal narrative around Mondays doesn't help either. If you look around, there are countless memes, jokes, and conversations that paint Monday as the villain of the week. This collective cultural mindset inevitably influences our perception, adding a layer of dread to the start of the week.

Another contributing factor to the Monday Blues is a lack of engagement or satisfaction with one's job. If you're not feeling fulfilled or challenged in your role, returning to it each week can feel like a difficult task. It's not just about disliking your job; sometimes, it's about not seeing how your work aligns with your broader life goals or values.

The impact of relaxation over the weekend can't be understated either. While rest is essential, a significant change in our sleep schedule or indulgence in activities that aren't part of our weekly routine (think late nights or social gatherings) can disrupt our biological clock. The term 'social jetlag' captures this phenomenon well, illustrating how these shifts can leave us feeling out of sync come Monday morning.

Similarly, the concept of "Sunday Scaries" is worth understanding. This term refers to the anxiety that begins on Sunday as the reality of the upcoming week sets in. It's a mix of anticipatory anxiety and a reflection of not feeling ready to face what's ahead, further cementing the challenge of Mondays.

Of course, health habits play a significant role as well. Studies suggest that we're more likely to engage in unhealthy behaviors over the weekend, such as binge eating or increased alcohol consumption. These habits can lead to feeling sluggish or emotionally unwell at the start of the week, exacerbating the difficulties of transitioning back into work.

On a physiological level, our bodies are also adjusting. Hormone levels, including cortisol, fluctuate based on our stress levels and activities. After two days of potentially different routines, our bodies have to readjust, not just to the work mindset but to the physical demands of our job.

Job dissatisfaction or a sense of burnout compounds these factors significantly. Feeling undervalued, overwhelmed, or stuck in your job are sensations that don't just disappear over the weekend. They simmer beneath the surface, contributing to the sense of dread that many associate with Monday.

Moreover, cognitive distortions, or the way we perceive our realities, are magnified when facing a situation we're inclined to view negatively. If we're predisposed to seeing Monday as a hurdle, our minds will highlight every minor inconvenience or stressor, making the day seem even worse.

For many, underlying issues such as anxiety and depression also play a crucial role in how they experience Mondays. These aren't just bad days; they're symptomatic of deeper challenges that need addressing, far beyond what a better Sunday routine can fix.

However, understanding the myriad reasons for the Monday Blues is the first step toward overcoming them. It's about recognizing that while the day of the week can't change, our approach to it can. Empowerment comes from acknowledging these challenges and actively seeking strategies to mitigate them, a subject we dive into deeply in the following chapters.

The reasons behind the Monday Blues are complex and multifaceted. They stem from a mix of societal influences, personal habits, job satisfaction levels, and even biological factors. Recognizing the interplay of these elements offers valuable insights into why we face these blues and, importantly, how we can begin to address them.

As we move forward, keep in mind that it's not about eradicating these feelings overnight, but understanding and navigating them with compassion and intention. Improving our Mondays, and by extension our work-life balance and job performance, is a journey worth undertaking. Together, we'll explore strategies to transform the Monday Blues from a dreaded certainty into an opportunity for growth and positivity.

Not Wanting the Weekend to Be Over

Many of us have been there, feeling that wave of dread as Sunday evening draws to a close, signaling the end of the weekend and the looming presence of Monday. This sentiment is a core aspect of the Monday Blues, deeply entangled with our desire to hold onto the freedom and relaxation the weekend represents. It's not just about disliking our jobs or our responsibilities; it's also about the stark contrast between the autonomy of our weekend schedules and the structured demands of the workweek.

The reluctance to let go of the weekend can stem from various sources. For some, weekends are a precious time to pursue hobbies, spend time with loved ones, or simply rest. The thought of transitioning back to work can feel like a jolt to this temporary but cherished freedom. For others, the issue might not be with work itself but with what it symbolizes—the loss of personal time, the pressure of deadlines, and the potential for workplace stress.

This resistance to the end of the weekend also echoes a broader struggle with work-life balance. It's a reminder that, for many, the scale tips heavily towards work, leaving little time for personal pursuits or relaxation. This imbalance can make weekends feel all the more precious and the transition to Monday all the more difficult. It's about the mental shift from doing what we love, or simply resting, to gearing up for the challenges and demands of the workweek.

Understanding this resistance is crucial in tackling the Monday Blues. It's not merely about Sunday night anxiety; it's about acknowledging the deeper discontent with how we allocate our time between work and personal life. It calls for a reassessment of how we view our work, our time, and our priorities. By framing Monday not as the end of something good but as the beginning of a productive week, we can start to shift our perspective and perhaps even find aspects of our work that we can look forward to.

Ultimately, it's about cultivating a mindset that views Mondays—and by extension, our work—with a sense of purpose and positivity. This doesn't mean dismissing the value of our weekends or the legitimate concerns about work-life balance. Instead, it's about finding a balance that allows us to transition from Sunday to Monday with less dread and more optimism. It's a journey that begins with acknowledging our feelings about the weekend ending and asking ourselves what changes we can make to start the week on a brighter note.

Transitions Can Be Hard

Let's face it, transitioning from the freedom and leisure of the weekend back into the structured routine of a workweek can be tough. This jarring shift, from what feels like a personal space and time back to a controlled schedule dictated by work obligations, can be a significant source of the Monday blues many of us experience. It's more than just not wanting the weekend to end; it's about the stark contrast between two very different modes of living that happens overnight. The ease with which you can dive into your hobbies and passions or spend time with loved ones suddenly gives way to deadlines, emails, and responsibilities. It's no wonder that the transition can feel so difficult.

This challenging transition is not just an emotional response but has tangible effects on our well-being and job performance. It's akin to a mini culture shock every week. Your mind and body, settled into a more relaxed rhythm, suddenly need to gear up for the heightened demands of the workweek. This shift can cause a mix of anxiety, lethargy, and even a sense of loss each Sunday night and Monday morning. It's a cycle that feels hard to escape, feeding into a loop of dread that can start as early as Sunday afternoon for some.

Understanding that transitions can be hard is the first step toward mitigating their impact. Acknowledging the struggle allows us to give ourselves a bit of grace. It's perfectly normal to feel this way, and it doesn't mean you're failing or falling behind. It means you're human, and like all humans, changes, especially abrupt ones, can take a toll on you. By recognizing this, we can begin to approach Mondays with a strategy, rather than letting them loom large and ominous in our minds.

What's important is how we manage these transitions. Small steps like preparing for Monday on Friday, setting up a Sunday evening routine that eases you into the work mindset, or even redefining what Mondays mean to you can make a big difference. These strategies can act as a bridge, making the passage from weekend to workweek less daunting. It's about creating a softer landing for Monday, rather than a harsh return to reality.

Ultimately, the way we perceive and interact with our Mondays can shift. It may never be your favorite day of the week, but it doesn't have to be the worst. With intention and effort, the sharp edges of this weekly transition can be smoothed out. It's about creating a balance that acknowledges the challenges while also embracing strategies that can lessen the impact. Transitioning from weekend to workweek can be made softer, proving that with the right mindset and tools, we can conquer even the toughest of Monday blues.

Statistically, Workers Are Unhealthier on Mondays

Welcome to a fascinating glimpse into how the dreaded Monday blues may be impacting more than just our moods – they might also be affecting our health. It's a phenomenon that has puzzled researchers and workers alike, sparking a series of studies aimed at understanding why, statistically, workers tend to be unhealthier on Mondays.

The beginning of the workweek seems to carry a heavy load, and it's not just the influx of emails or the piled-up tasks that contribute to this dread. Intriguingly, research reveals a spike in health-related complaints and absences from work on Mondays. This pattern suggests a correlation that extends beyond mere coincidence, prompting a closer examination of the underlying causes.

One plausible explanation lies in the drastic shift in our lifestyle habits over the weekend. For many, weekends are a time for relaxation, indulgence, and staying up late, which starkly contrasts with the structured routine of the workweek. This sudden change can shock the system, manifesting in both physical and psychological discomfort on Mondays.

Heart-related issues exemplify this trend, with studies indicating an increase in heart attacks and strokes early in the week. Experts believe that the stress associated with the transition back to work plays a critical role in this uptick, highlighting the profound impact of work-related stress on our physical well-being.

Beyond the cardiovascular implications, there's also a notable rise in gastrointestinal complaints on Mondays. The excesses of the weekend, be it in terms of diet or alcohol consumption, can aggravate conditions like acid reflux and indigestion, leading to higher absenteeism rates at the start of the week.

Moreover, the psychological toll of Mondays can't be ignored. The dread of returning to work can exacerbate symptoms of anxiety and depression, making it harder for individuals to get out of bed and face the day. This mental health aspect is crucial, as it can influence physical health and overall well-being.

Interestingly, sleep patterns play a significant role in the Monday health dilemma. Disruptions in our sleep schedule over the weekend – a phenomenon known as social jetlag – leave many feeling groggy and out of sorts when Monday rolls around. The lack of quality sleep can weaken the immune system, making us more susceptible to illness.

Chronic conditions, too, seem to flare up at the beginning of the week. Patients with arthritis and migraines, for example, report increased severity in their symptoms on Mondays. This could be attributed to a combination of poor sleep, increased stress, and dietary indiscretions over the weekend.

But it's not all doom and gloom. While the data paints a somber picture, it also offers valuable insights into how we can mitigate these health risks. For instance, maintaining a consistent sleep schedule and moderating weekend indulgence can help ease the transition into the workweek.

Furthermore, workplace interventions aimed at reducing Monday stress could play a pivotal role in enhancing employee health. Initiatives like flexible scheduling, reduced workload, and wellness programs can help create a more supportive environment that eases the Monday blues and their accompanying health concerns.

Understanding the factors that contribute to worse health on Mondays is the first step toward countering them. Employers and employees alike can benefit from acknowledging these patterns and working collaboratively to promote healthier habits and work practices.

The conversation about health and well-being in the workplace is evolving, and recognizing the unique challenges posed by Mondays is crucial. By addressing these issues head-on, we can foster a culture of health that extends beyond the workplace, improving overall quality of life for everyone.

As we delve deeper into the subsequent chapters, we'll explore practical strategies and tips for overcoming the Monday blues, enhancing our work-life balance, and boosting job performance. It's about making Mondays not just bearable, but productive and enjoyable, transforming the beginning of the week from a health risk to an opportunity for positive engagement and well-being.

The phenomenon of workers being unhealthier on Mondays serves as a reminder of the intricate interplay between our work lives and our health. By taking proactive steps to understand and address the root causes of the Monday blues, we can pave the way for a healthier, happier, and more productive work environment for all.

Binge Eating and Drinking

Let's talk about a widespread issue that plays a critical yet often underestimated role in the dreaded Monday blues: binge eating and drinking over the weekend. It's a cycle that's as damaging as it is common, and it intricately feeds into the despair many feel at the start of the workweek.

Many of us fall into the trap of using food and alcohol as coping mechanisms to either celebrate the weekend's freedom or to numb the dread of the upcoming Monday. It starts innocently enough — a dinner out here, a few drinks there. But before you know it, the weekend spirals into a cycle of overindulgence that leaves you feeling physically sluggish and mentally clouded by the time Monday rolls around.

This pattern, deeply intertwined with our attempts to maximize weekend pleasure, unfortunately, leads to significant spikes in guilt, anxiety, and even depression. And here's the kicker — the mental fog and physical discomfort aren't just fleeting annoyances. They pave the way for a spectrum of negative emotions that color your perception of the upcoming week.

Consider how a heavy meal loaded with carbohydrates and fats can make you feel. Initially, there's the comfort, the sensory pleasure. But this soon turns into lethargy and sluggishness. Alcohol, on the other hand, may initially seem like it's lifting your spirits. In reality, it's a depressant that can exacerbate feelings of sadness and anxiety as its effects wane.

More than just affecting your mood, these patterns interrupt your body's natural rhythms. Your sleep, crucial for emotional and physical restoration, gets disrupted. The intricacies of sleep are significant — it's not just about duration, but quality. Alcohol, especially, is notorious for impairing sleep quality, leading to a restless night and, subsequently, a groggy morning.

Now, layers of guilt often accompany the realization of these weekend excesses. There's a societal narrative that equates self-control with virtue and excess with a lack of discipline. Thus, Monday doesn't just become a return to work; it turns into a day of penance, where the perceived 'sins' of the weekend need to be atoned for.

It's easy to see how eating and drinking excessively can be symptomatic of deeper issues. Perhaps it's dissatisfaction with work, the overwhelming nature of our responsibilities, or even deeper mental health struggles. The weekend becomes a brief escape, a momentary break from reality, before the inevitable crash.

But here's the thing — breaking this cycle is integral to not only improving how we face Mondays but enhancing our overall quality of life. It starts with mindfulness, recognizing the why behind our actions. It's about confronting the fact that while food and drink can bring temporary solace, they're not solutions to underlying problems.

Making conscious choices about how we spend our weekends means actively seeking alternatives that nourish rather than deplete us. It's about finding balance, perhaps trading in that extra drink for a walk or swapping the binge-eating for a cooking session that engages your senses in a healthier way.

This doesn't mean you shouldn't indulge or enjoy yourself. It's about moderation and recognizing that true relaxation and joy don't come from extremes. They come from balance, from activities that rejuvenate rather than exhaust us mentally and physically.

Moreover, reframing the way we view Mondays can significantly impact our weekend choices. If we see Monday not as an end but a beginning, a chance to implement positive changes and pursue meaningful goals, weekends become less about escaping and more about refreshing and preparing.

Practicing self-compassion is also critical. If you did indulge over the weekend, avoid beating yourself up. Instead, focus on what you can do differently moving forward. Small, incremental changes often lead to significant, lasting impacts.

Remember, the aim isn't to remove all pleasure from the weekend. It's to cultivate a relationship with food and drink that enriches our lives rather than complicating them. It's to enjoy these pleasures in a way that leaves us feeling good come Monday, not just momentarily gratified but genuinely refreshed and ready for the week ahead.

So, as we navigate the complex interplay between our weekend activities and the Monday blues, let's strive for balance and mindfulness. Let's make choices that honor our bodies and minds, fostering a healthier, happier start to each week. In doing so, we rewrite the narrative of Mondays, transforming them from a day of dread to one of opportunity and new beginnings.

Sleep Pattern Changes

As we delve deeper into understanding the Monday blues, it's crucial to turn our attention to one of the most significant, yet often overlooked, contributors: sleep pattern changes. The rhythm of our workweek and weekend activities tends to disrupt our natural sleep cycles, setting the stage for the unease many of us feel as Monday approaches.

The concept is simple yet profound. During the week, routines dictate our bedtime and wake-up schedules, creating a semblance of regularity. Yet, as the weekend arrives, the sudden freedom to sleep in or stay up later disrupts this rhythm. This alteration in sleep patterns over the weekend doesn't just affect our alertness but profoundly impacts our mood and overall well-being, making the transition into Monday feel more jarring.

Consider how a typical weekend might unfold. The relief and excitement of Friday evening often lead to staying up later than usual, reveling in the freedom from early alarms. Saturday might follow a similar pattern, further distancing us from our weekly routine. Sleeping in on these days feels like a luxury, yet it significantly shifts our internal clock, making Sunday night's return to 'normal' sleep time challenging.

This shift, often referred to as "social jet lag," creates a mismatch between our body's biological clock and our social clock, the schedule we live by due to work or social commitments. The effects can be likened to flying across time zones without leaving your home, resulting in similar symptoms to traditional jet lag such as fatigue, irritability, and difficulty concentrating.

What's more, disrupted sleep patterns impact our physical health too. Studies have shown that inconsistent sleep can affect our immune system, metabolism, and even our heart health. This interplay between physical and mental well-being can exacerbate feelings of dread and discomfort associated with Mondays, making it not just a matter of insufficient rest but of holistic health.

Beyond the physical, there's a psychological component. The abrupt shift from weekend freedom to the structured demands of Monday can make the day feel particularly oppressive. It's not just the activities of the day that weigh on us but the sudden change in how we feel physically, largely influenced by how we've slept.

Addressing these sleep pattern changes requires mindfulness and deliberate planning. Establishing a more consistent sleep schedule that aligns closely with our natural circadian rhythms can mitigate the effects of social jet lag. While it might be tempting to indulge in late nights over the weekend, gradually adjusting our sleep time by an hour or less can make a significant difference.

Practicing good sleep hygiene is also essential. This includes maintaining a comfortable and quiet sleep environment, avoiding screens and heavy meals before bedtime, and engaging in relaxing activities such as reading or taking a bath. These habits can help signal to our body that it's time to wind down, easing the transition into sleep.

Nutrition and exercise play supportive roles in this process as well. A balanced diet and regular physical activity can improve sleep quality and help regulate our internal clock. By taking care of our body, we're laying the groundwork for better sleep and, by extension, smoother transitions into the working week.

The impact of light exposure on our sleep patterns cannot be overstated. The blue light emanating from screens can interfere with our body's production of melatonin, the hormone responsible for regulating sleep. Limiting screen time in the evening and increasing exposure to natural light during the day can help realign our sleep patterns.

Moreover, engaging in relaxation techniques such as mindfulness meditation or deep breathing exercises before bedtime can also improve sleep quality. These practices not only help in falling asleep more easily but also enhance the quality of rest, making it more restorative.

For those who find it particularly challenging to adjust their sleep patterns, consulting with a healthcare provider or a sleep specialist may be beneficial. There can be underlying issues such as sleep disorders that, once addressed, significantly improve one's ability to rest effectively.

In essence, the Monday blues aren't merely a mindset issue; they're deeply intertwined with our physical well-being, with sleep pattern changes playing a pivotal role. It's a reminder that taking care of our body's needs is a critical component of improving our work-life balance and job performance.

Embracing a more mindful approach to our weekend sleep habits doesn't mean sacrificing our freedom for enjoyment. It's about finding balance, acknowledging the profound impact of rest on our physical and emotional state, and making small adjustments to support our overall well-being. As we slowly reshape our sleep habits, the dread of Mondays can diminish, making way for a more balanced, productive, and joyful start to the week.

Ultimately, our sleep patterns are a key piece of the puzzle in understanding and combating the Monday blues. By prioritizing regular, restorative rest, we equip ourselves with the resilience needed to face Mondays with a renewed sense of energy and optimism. It's a gentle yet powerful reminder that our best days start with a good night's sleep.

Hormone Levels

Welcome to the chapter on hormone levels, a crucial, yet often overlooked aspect of the infamous Monday Blues. You might be wondering what hormones have to do with the feeling of dread that accompanies the start of the workweek. The answer lies in the complex way our body's internal chemistry reacts to external pressures and routine changes, especially as we transition from the freedom of the weekend back to the structured environment of work.

It's important to understand that hormones are powerful chemicals produced by glands in the endocrine system. They flow through the bloodstream, acting as messengers affecting various processes in the body, including mood regulation. Among these, cortisol, often dubbed the "stress hormone," plays a significant role in how we feel throughout the week.

Over the weekend, our cortisol levels can vary significantly. Many of us sleep more, eat differently, and perhaps enjoy more social activities than during the week. This change in routine can affect our body's rhythm and hormonal balance. Come Monday, when the alarm goes off earlier and the pace of life quickens, our cortisol levels spike, preparing us for the "fight or flight" response to the stress of returning to work.

Additionally, serotonin, a hormone and neurotransmitter associated with feelings of happiness and well-being, shows fluctuating levels that correlate with our mood swings. During the weekend, activities that we enjoy can increase serotonin production, which might explain the relative peace and happiness we feel. However, the anticipation or arrival of Monday can disrupt this balance, leading to feelings of melancholy or the Monday Blues.

Dopamine, another neurotransmitter linked to the brain's reward system, plays a role too. Activities over the weekend that bring us joy and relaxation increase dopamine levels, giving us a sense of pleasure and reward. Yet, the sharp contrast of Monday and its demands can result in a significant drop in dopamine, making the start of the workweek feel particularly unrewarding and challenging.

This hormonal turbulence is not merely about feeling a little off as we start the week. It can have tangible effects on our physical and emotional well-being. Higher cortisol levels can lead to increased stress, anxiety, and even physical health issues over time, such as high blood pressure and a weakened immune system.

The good news is that by understanding these hormonal influences, we can develop strategies to mitigate their impact. For instance, stabilizing our weekend sleep schedule to more closely match our weekday routine can help moderate cortisol fluctuations. Similarly, incorporating activities that bring joy and satisfaction into our Sunday evenings and Monday mornings can help maintain more consistent serotonin and dopamine levels.

It's also worth noting that our diet plays a significant role in our hormonal balance. Foods high in refined sugars and caffeine can spike cortisol levels, exacerbating stress and anxiety. Conversely, a balanced diet rich in omega-3 fatty acids, antioxidants, and fiber can support a more stable hormonal environment, helping to ease the transition into the workweek.

Regular physical activity is another powerful tool. Exercise stimulates the production of endorphins, often referred to as the body's natural painkillers and mood elevators. These hormones can counteract the effects of increased cortisol, providing a natural mood boost that can help smooth over the rough edges of Monday.

Moreover, mindfulness and relaxation techniques, such as meditation or deep-breathing exercises, can influence hormonal balance by activating the body's relaxation response. This can help lower cortisol levels, reducing stress and improving our overall mood as we face the week ahead.

Developing a supportive social network can also make a difference. Interacting with friends and loved ones can increase levels of oxytocin, sometimes called the "love hormone," which has a calming effect and can counteract stress hormones. Even planning a lunch date or a brief Monday morning check-in with a friend can lend a much-needed boost.

Importantly, individual differences mean that there's no one-size-fits-all solution. It's beneficial to pay attention to how your body and mood vary with your activities, routines, and dietary choices throughout the week. This awareness will allow you to make more informed decisions that support hormonal balance, helping to mitigate the Monday Blues.

While hormones are but one piece of the puzzle when it comes to understanding and overcoming the Monday Blues, they play a significant role. By taking steps to maintain a more stable hormonal balance, we can improve not only our Mondays but our overall sense of well-being and productivity throughout the week. Remember, small changes in our daily routines can have a profound impact on our hormonal health and, by extension, our happiness and fulfillment in both our personal and professional lives.

Job Dissatisfaction or Burnout

Many of us have faced mornings where the thought of going to work seems unbearable, not because we're inherently lazy or opposed to work, but because our jobs no longer ignite that spark within us. This feeling can stem from a variety of sources, but predominantly, job dissatisfaction and burnout are culprits that transform our Sundays into dread-filled preludes to Monday.

Burnout doesn't appear out of nowhere. It's a gradual process, one that creeps up on us as slowly and silently as shadows at dusk. It often starts with the nagging feeling that our work doesn't matter, that despite our efforts, we're not making a dent in the universe, or worse, in our own lives.

Job dissatisfaction, on the other hand, can be a bit more complex. It can arise from feeling undervalued or underpaid, working in a toxic environment, or simply being misaligned with the company's values or tasks assigned. It's that constant whisper in the back of your mind, questioning if this is truly how you want to spend a significant portion of your life.

These feelings of discontent and exhaustion are not just mental states; they have physical manifestations. From the moment the alarm rings on Monday, your body might protest, making it a major effort to get out of bed. This lethargy isn't just about being tired; it's your physical self signaling that something's amiss in your professional life.

When discussing burnout, it's essential to highlight the role of continuous stress. It's like having your foot on the gas pedal non-stop, without any destination in sight. Eventually, the fuel runs out – or in our case, our mental, emotional, and physical reserves. The once vibrant enthusiasm we had for our work dims, leaving us feeling empty and spent.

Ironically, the harder we work under these conditions, the less effective we become. Our productivity plummets, not because we aren't trying, but because we're operating from a depleted state. It's a vicious cycle: we push harder to compensate for the dip in performance, which only exacerbates our exhaustion and dissatisfaction.

One of the most deceptive aspects of burnout is its ability to make us feel isolated. It's as if we're the only ones struggling while everyone else seems to have it all figured out. This isolation is not just imagined; it's often physical, as we start withdrawing from colleagues and work activities, further deepening the chasm between us and our work environment.

Recognizing the signs of job dissatisfaction and burnout is the first step towards addressing them. These can include constant fatigue, irritability, a feeling of detachment from your job, a decrease in job performance, and the sensation that no matter what you do, it's never enough.

But it's not all doom and gloom. The beauty of hitting this low is the profound clarity it brings about what we don't want. It's an opportunity to reassess our career paths and realign our jobs with our values, talents, and passions. Sometimes, the realization that we've outgrown our roles can be the catalyst for profound personal and professional growth.

Addressing job dissatisfaction and burnout requires a multi-pronged approach. It might entail having candid conversations with supervisors about our feelings and seeking their support for possible solutions. This could include workload adjustments, exploring new roles within the organization, or even pursuing professional development opportunities that reignite our passion for our work.

Self-care also plays a crucial role in combating burnout. This extends beyond the cliched spa days to encompass mindful practices like setting clear work-life boundaries, engaging in regular physical activity, and prioritizing activities that rejuvenate us both mentally and physically.

Networking shouldn't be underestimated either. Connecting with peers, both within and outside our current organizations, can provide new perspectives, empathy from those who've traversed similar paths, and sometimes, opportunities for a fresh start elsewhere.

Ultimately, overcoming job dissatisfaction and burnout is a journey towards finding meaning and satisfaction in our work again. It's about rediscovering that spark that not only makes Mondays bearable but transforms them into something we might even look forward to. It's a testament to our resilience and our unwavering quest for a fulfilling professional life.

While the path to overcoming job dissatisfaction and burnout is rarely linear or easy, it's fraught with opportunities for self-discovery and growth. By acknowledging our feelings, taking proactive steps to address them, and remembering that our worth is not defined by our productivity, we can slowly but surely rekindle our passion for our work and perhaps, in the process, rediscover ourselves.

So, let's view the Monday Blues not as a dreaded affliction but as a wake-up call, reminding us to periodically check in with ourselves and ensure that our jobs are still in alignment with who we are and who we aspire to be. By doing so, we transform our relationship with work from one of mere survival to one of thriving and fulfillment.

Cognitive Distortions

Cognitive distortions, the mind's way of playing tricks on us, lead many into the trap of the Monday Blues. At its core, these distortions are patterns of negative thinking that make our realities seem worse than they actually are. Understanding how these distortions contribute to our dread of Mondays can be the first step in overcoming them.

One common distortion is "all-or-nothing thinking," where we see our experiences in black and white. For example, if a project doesn't go perfectly, you might feel like the entire week is ruined, just because it's Monday. This mindset amplifies the stress and pressure of starting the week.

Another distortion is "overgeneralization." Let's say you had a rough Monday last week. If you're overgeneralizing, you might conclude that all Mondays will be just as bad, setting a negative tone before the week has even begun. Every Monday becomes a self-fulfilling prophecy of doom and gloom, regardless of the actual circumstances.

"Filtering" is when we magnify negative details of our experiences and filter out all positive aspects. If you're focusing on how much you dread getting up early for work on Monday, you might completely overlook the enjoyment of your morning coffee or the satisfaction of completing tasks.

Then there's "catastrophizing," where the mere thought of Monday spirals into exaggerated worst-case scenarios. A simple meeting scheduled for a Monday morning can loom in your mind as a career-defining moment of doom, increasing your anxiety and distaste for Mondays.

"Jumping to conclusions" is also prevalent when facing the Monday Blues. This involves mind reading, where you presume to know what others are thinking, and fortune telling, where you predict future events negatively. You might assume that your boss will be in a bad mood on Monday or that something will go wrong, without any real evidence to support these beliefs.

It's also useful to consider "emotional reasoning," which is when you believe something to be true because it feels true. If you feel a sense of dread as Sunday night rolls around, you might take this feeling as proof that Monday will be terrible, even if it's just the usual start to the workweek.

"Should statements" are another distortion that can exacerbate the Monday Blues. Telling yourself what you should or shouldn't feel or do creates a pressure that amplifies anxiety. For instance, thinking "I shouldn't feel so anxious about Mondays" can lead to guilt, making the situation worse.

Engaging in "labeling and mislabeling" involves attaching negative labels to ourselves or others without considering the situation accurately. If you label yourself as "lazy" just because you're struggling to get out of bed on Monday, you're not giving yourself a fair chance.

"Personalization" occurs when we blame ourselves for events outside our control. If something goes wrong at the beginning of the week, you might unfairly hold yourself responsible, adding undeserved stress to your Mondays.

Understanding cognitive distortions gives us power over them. Recognizing these patterns as distortions rather than truths can help relieve the intensity of the Monday Blues. Shifting your perspective is key; instead of viewing Monday as a looming giant, we can start to see it as just another day, with both potential challenges and rewards.

Combatting these distortions begins with mindfulness and reflection. Acknowledging that your dread of Mondays may be amplified by cognitive distortions is a step toward reprogramming your thoughts. Rather than accepting your initial negative thoughts about Monday, challenge them. Ask yourself if they're truly accurate or if they're examples of distorted thinking.

Beyond individual reflection, discussing your feelings and thoughts with others can bring new perspectives that challenge your cognitive distortions. Sometimes it takes another person pointing out the brighter side of things to see beyond our negative filters.

Creating a Monday ritual can also counteract cognitive distortions. By establishing positive associations with Monday, like a special breakfast or an enjoyable morning playlist, you can begin to dismantle the automatic negative associations your mind jumps to.

In essence, the journey to mitigating Monday blues involves recognizing and addressing the cognitive distortions at play. With conscious effort, we can reframe our thoughts and start our weeks not with dread but with a balanced perspective, acknowledging challenges but also embracing opportunities. By doing so, we reclaim our Mondays and, by extension, our sense of joy and productivity in our work and personal lives.

Anxiety and Depression

At the heart of the Monday blues lies an intricate web of feelings, among which anxiety and depression often weave their most complex patterns. For many, the transition from the freedom and respite of the weekend into the structured demands of the workweek triggers more than just a transient sense of dread. It ignites a deeper, more profound struggle, where the onset of the week becomes symbolic of broader emotional battles.

The relationship between workplace stress and mental health has been well-documented, yet its nuances can't be overstated. Anxiety, with its clammy hands of worry, often grips individuals as Sunday night approaches, morphing their anticipation of challenges into a paralyzing fear of what's to come. This isn't merely about facing a pile of unattended emails or a series of meetings. It's about confronting a reality that feels overwhelming and occasionally insurmountable.

Depression, on the other hand, casts a longer, deeper shadow over one's experience of the workweek's start. It can diminish the color of life to monochromatic hues, turning even the most passionate endeavors into pointless tasks. Here, the Monday blues transform into an abyss, where motivation and vitality are consumed by an all-encompassing bleakness.

Yet, understanding these experiences requires more than just acknowledging their existence. It demands a compassionate, nuanced exploration of how our work environment and personal expectations interplay with our mental health. For many, the dread of Mondays is not simply about the day itself but about what it represents — a lack of fulfillment, a misalignment of values, or the feeling of being stuck in a cycle that does not resonate with one's aspirations.

The narrative of anxiety and depression within the context of the Monday blues is not one of weakness. It is a testament to the complexities of the human experience, a reminder that our work lives are not separate from our emotional selves. It is crucial, therefore, to approach this topic not merely as a matter of productivity but as an essential aspect of personal well-being.

In addressing anxiety and depression, the focus often shifts towards individual coping mechanisms. While such strategies are invaluable, it's also essential to zoom out and consider systemic factors playing a role. The modern workplace, with its often unrelenting pace, expectation of constant connectivity, and the blurring lines between personal and professional life, can serve as a breeding ground for mental health challenges.

Thus, mitigating the Monday blues, particularly for those grappling with anxiety and depression, requires a multifaceted approach. It involves creating spaces where conversations about mental health are welcomed and destigmatized. It calls for personal reflection on our relationship with our work and an honest assessment of how it aligns with our deeper values and needs.

An important aspect of this journey is the recognition that you're not alone. The very fact that the term "Monday blues" is a prevalent part of our language points to a shared understanding—an acknowledgment that the start of the work week can be particularly challenging. This offers a foundation for solidarity, for shared narratives that can catalyze change, both within workplaces and within ourselves.

For individuals struggling with anxiety and depression, this realization can be both a source of comfort and a call to action. It's about recognizing that while your experiences are deeply personal, they are also part of a larger cultural and societal fabric. This dual perspective can empower individuals to seek support, whether through therapy, community, or changes in their work environment.

In practical terms, addressing anxiety and depression as they relate to the Monday blues involves both short-term strategies to ease the transition into the workweek and long-term efforts to cultivate a healthier relationship with work. This might include setting boundaries around work hours, incorporating routines that bolster well-being, and seeking professional help when necessary.

It also involves a critical examination of workplace culture. Employers play a crucial role in this equation, with the potential to foster environments that prioritize mental health, offer flexibility, and recognize the importance of life beyond work. This not only benefits employees but can enhance productivity, creativity, and loyalty—transforming the dread of Monday into an opportunity for growth and innovation.

The journey towards reconciling our work lives with our mental health is ongoing and evolving. It requires patience, courage, and a willingness to confront uncomfortable truths. Yet, it's a journey filled with potential for transformation—not just of our individual experiences, but of our collective understanding of work, well-being, and the intricate dance between the two.

Ultimately, the Monday blues, particularly when intertwined with anxiety and depression, invite us to engage in deeper introspection about what truly matters to us. They challenge us to envision a world where our work not only sustains us financially but nurtures our spirits, aligns with our values, and contributes to a sense of meaning and fulfillment.

This vision is not just a distant dream but a possibility that becomes more tangible as we navigate the complexities of our work-life balance with awareness, compassion, and resilience. By disentangling the threads of anxiety and depression from our experience of Mondays, we open ourselves up to a fuller, more vibrant understanding of both ourselves and the potential for our work lives to be a source of joy rather than distress.

In confronting the Monday blues head-on, particularly through the lens of mental health, we're not just seeking to survive the start of the workweek. We're striving to thrive, to rebuild our relationship with our work in a way that honors our well-being and celebrates our humanity. It's a bold, brave journey—one that redefines the meaning of success and challenges us to find harmony in the fragile balance between work and life.

Chapter 2:
The Impact of Monday Blues on Work-Life Harmony

Mondays often come with their unique set of challenges and blues, casting a long shadow over our work-life harmony. When we find ourselves trapped in the cycle of dreading Mondays, it's not just a fleeting feeling but a phenomenon that can significantly affect our overall well-being and job performance. It's essential to recognize the gravity of this issue, as the ripple effect touches all corners of our lives.

First and foremost, the impact on personal well-being cannot be overstated. Monday blues often stem from a variety of sources, including the abrupt transition from the freedom of the weekend to the structure of the workweek, sleep pattern disruptions, and even deeper issues like job dissatisfaction. This cocktail of factors contributes to a decline in mental health, causing heightened stress, anxiety, and even depression in severe cases.

The consequences extend into our physical health as well. The stress associated with starting the workweek can lead to an increase in cortisol levels, making us more susceptible to health problems such as hypertension and weakened immune response. Moreover, the somber mood of Mondays often leads individuals to neglect physical activity, opting instead for comfort foods that might offer temporary solace but contribute to long-term health issues.

When it comes to job performance, the ripple effect of Monday blues shows no mercy here either. Starting the week with low energy and a lack of motivation can set a negative tone for the days to follow. Productivity suffers as tasks take longer to complete and the quality of work may decline. Creativity and innovation, often the bedrock of professional advancement, become casualties of this dispirited state.

Furthermore, the atmosphere within the workplace takes a hit. When many employees are experiencing Monday blues, it creates a collective lethargy that can dampen even the most vibrant work cultures. The sense of camaraderie and teamwork necessary for a flourishing work environment can erode, making it harder for everyone to achieve their goals.

Personal relationships are not immune to the effects of Monday blues either. The stress and irritability carried over from work can impact our interactions with loved ones, creating a cycle of negativity that affects our home life as well. This exacerbates the stress we feel, creating a feedback loop that makes finding work-life balance all the more challenging.

Beyond the immediate effects on work and personal life, the undercurrent of Monday blues can erode our sense of purpose and fulfillment. When our workweek starts on a low note, it's easy to lose sight of our goals and the bigger picture of why we do what we do. This lack of purpose can lead to disengagement and dissatisfaction at work, which only feeds into the cycle of dread that comes with each approaching Monday.

Leveraging this awareness into action is crucial. Recognizing the toll Monday blues take on our work-life harmony is the first step towards mitigating their impact. It involves a holistic approach, addressing the symptoms as well as the root causes. This may mean making adjustments in our personal lives, such as establishing better sleep hygiene or dedicating time to unwind and prepare mentally for the week ahead.

In the realm of work, it may involve seeking job satisfaction by engaging in tasks that bring a sense of accomplishment and purpose. Being proactive about managing workload and stress levels can also make a significant difference in how we approach Mondays.

It's important to break the myth that Monday blues are an inevitable part of working life. They are a signal, not a sentence. By listening to what these feelings are trying to tell us about our needs, whether personal or professional, we can begin to counteract them. It's about creating a life where Mondays are no longer a day to dread but an opportunity for growth and positivity.

Creating a Monday morning ritual that we look forward to can act as a powerful antidote to the blues. Whether it's a workout, a special breakfast, or time set aside for reflection and planning, having a ritual can transform our outlook for the day.

Moreover, the role of employers in this equation cannot be understated. A supportive work environment that acknowledges the Monday blues by offering flexibility, promoting a positive culture, and encouraging work-life balance can make a tremendous difference. Employers have the opportunity to lead by example, showing that it's not just the responsibility of the individual to combat the Monday blues but a collective effort.

As we delve deeper into the strategies to eliminate Monday blues in the coming chapters, remember that striving for work-life harmony is a continuous process. It's about making small, sustainable changes that lead to significant improvements over time. By addressing the impact of Monday blues head-on, we open the door to not only better Mondays but a more fulfilling work-life journey.

The Monday blues don't have to define our experience of work and life. With awareness, proactivity, and support, it's possible to transform the way we view and approach our Mondays. Let us focus on creating a life where balance, fulfillment, and positivity guide our way, making every day, including Monday, an opportunity for joy and success.

Repercussions on Personal Well-Being

The phenomenon of Monday Blues is far from being a mere cultural or social meme that circulates around the start of each workweek. It's a real psychological pattern that directly impacts personal well-being, setting a tone that resonates throughout the week. Here, we delve into why understanding and addressing these feelings is crucial for maintaining a balanced life.

First and foremost, the sense of dread or unease that accompanies the end of the weekend can exacerbate feelings of anxiety and depression. This isn't just about facing a long week of work; it taps into deeper issues of job dissatisfaction, burnout, and a perceived lack of control over one's life and schedule. The transition from the freedom of the weekend to the structure of the workweek can feel like a loss, leading to emotional turmoil.

Moreover, the stress associated with Monday blues can take a toll on physical health. Elevated stress levels are linked with numerous health issues, including high blood pressure, weakened immune function, and increased risk of chronic diseases. The tension can also lead to muscle tightness, headaches, and gastrointestinal disturbances, conditions that hamper both work performance and overall quality of life.

Poor sleep patterns often accompany the dread of Monday, disrupting the body's natural rhythm. The attempt to catch up on sleep lost during the workweek by sleeping in on weekends creates what is known as 'social jet lag', worsening the feeling of unhappiness on Monday. This alteration in sleep patterns can affect cognition, mood, and physical health, further degrading personal well-being.

Another repercussion is the potential for unhealthy coping mechanisms. The strain of facing a new week may drive individuals towards binge eating, excessive alcohol consumption, or neglecting physical activity. Such habits not only fail to address the root cause of Monday Blues but also contribute to a cycle of poor health and reduced well-being.

The strain on personal relationships should not be underestimated. The irritability and mood swings that come with dread for Monday can strain interactions with loved ones, leading to conflicts or withdrawal, and thus isolating individuals from support systems crucial for personal well-being.

Furthermore, the anticipation of Monday can stifle personal growth and development. The mental energy consumed by dread and anxiety leaves little room for activities that promote personal enrichment, such as hobbies, learning, or socializing in meaningful ways. This stagnation can contribute to a sense of unfulfillment and dissatisfaction with life.

It's essential to recognize the impact of Monday Blues on work-life harmony. The imbalance created by dreading one-seventh of the week sets a negative precedent for achieving a fulfilling life. It emphasizes the importance of finding joy and purpose in one's work and life activities, a fundamental aspect of human fulfillment.

The cumulative effect of continuously facing Monday Blues can also lead to chronic stress. This ongoing state of tension exacerbates health risks, diminishes life satisfaction, and can precipitate or worsen mental health issues. The link between chronic stress and various forms of mental illness, including anxiety disorders and depression, highlights the importance of addressing the root causes of Monday Blues.

On a physiological level, chronic stress and anxiety triggered by the prospect of each workweek can disrupt hormonal balance. This disturbance affects moods, sleep, appetite, and overall physical health, creating a feedback loop that perpetuates feelings of unwellness and dread.

Financial well-being can also be indirectly affected. The lack of motivation and decreased productivity associated with Monday Blues can hinder career progression, impact job performance, and ultimately affect earnings and job security. This financial stress, in turn, exacerbates the sense of dread felt towards the workweek.

Additionally, the focus on the negative aspects of the workweek detracts from mindfulness and living in the present moment. An obsession with how challenging Monday will be can lead to missing out on the joy and relaxation that weekends are supposed to provide, leading to a life where one is always looking at the past or the future, never fully enjoying the now.

The personal well-being impact of Monday Blues also includes a diminished sense of accomplishment. When much of one's energy is focused on merely surviving the week, there's little left for setting and achieving personal goals, whether they're related to career, relationships, hobbies, or personal development. This can lead to feelings of stagnation and lack of progress in life.

Finally, it's worth noting that the dread of Mondays can make individuals feel isolated, as if they're the only ones struggling while everyone else seems to manage just fine. This perception of isolation can prevent seeking support or employing strategies to mitigate these feelings, further entrenching the cycle of Monday Blues.

Addressing the repercussions of Monday Blues on personal well-being is not about dismissing genuine concerns or emotions. It's about recognizing the profound impact they have on our lives and taking proactive steps to manage these feelings. The journey towards overcoming the dread of Mondays and fostering a healthier relationship with the workweek is a valuable investment in one's mental, physical, and emotional health, promising a more balanced and fulfilling life.

Impact on Job Performance

The start of the week always looms large in our collective consciousness, harboring the potential to set the tone for the days that follow. Certainly, the ripple effects of Monday blues stretch far and wide, influencing not just our personal well-being but also casting a sizable shadow over job performance. It's an often overlooked truth that how we feel on Monday can profoundly impact our effectiveness, creativity, and collaboration in the workplace.

Mondays tainted by a sense of dread or lack of motivation see a noticeable dip in employee engagement. When individuals are mentally checking the clock, counting the minutes until they can leave, their focus isn't on the task at hand. This disengagement doesn't just stifle productivity; it muffles the vibrant, innovative ideas that thrive in a more enthusiastic environment.

Then, consider the effects on time management. Starting the week off balance, struggling with Monday blues, often means an uphill battle to catch up on emails, projects, and meetings. Tasks that could normally be handled efficiently become burdensome, and the backlog continues to grow, creating a cycle of stress and inefficiency that can take days—or even the entire week—to resolve.

The quality of work also takes a hit. When our minds are clouded by the fog of Monday blues, attention to detail diminishes, and the care put into work projects is not what it could be. This drop in quality does not go unnoticed, potentially affecting team outcomes and individual assessments of competence and reliability.

Furthermore, the Monday blues can exacerbate communication issues. A person grappling with the lethargy and apathy that often accompany this state is less likely to seek out clarifications or engage in proactive communication. The result is an increase in misunderstandings and conflicts within teams, damaging the harmony and collaborative spirit essential for achieving shared goals.

Stress levels undeniably surge as well, not only from the backlog of work but from the emotional toll of battling through the day. This heightened stress is detrimental to both physical and mental health, leading to a cycle where each subsequent Monday feels even more daunting. The stress can manifest in physical symptoms, further impairing job performance and overall well-being.

Morale, an essential component of a thriving workplace, inevitably suffers. The contagious nature of emotions means one person's case of Monday blues can spread, dampening the enthusiasm and positivity of the entire team. When morale dips, so does the collective drive to push boundaries and strive for excellence.

A hidden casualty of the Monday blues is also innovation. When we're just trying to survive the day, there's little room left for the kind of out-of-the-box thinking that fuels progress. Creativity is stifled, and opportunities for growth and improvement pass by unnoticed.

In addition, customer service and client interactions can suffer. Employees facing a bout of Monday blues are less likely to deliver the level of service and engagement that customers expect. This can harm relationships with clients and potentially impact the company's reputation and bottom line.

Attendance issues frequently arise, with an increase in late arrivals and an uptick in sick days, as employees find it harder to motivate themselves to face the week. This disruption in consistency and reliability places additional strain on teams to cover for absent colleagues, further affecting productivity.

Furthermore, employee retention is at risk. Prolonged exposure to a cycle of dread and disengagement associated with Mondays leads to higher turnover rates. The costs of recruitment and training new employees, not to mention the loss of institutional knowledge and skills, can significantly impact an organization's stability and growth.

Leadership effectiveness is not immune to the impact of Monday blues either. Leaders struggling to find their footing at the start of the week may find it challenging to inspire and guide their teams effectively. Weakened leadership contributes to a lack of direction and motivation across the workforce.

The ripple effects extend to professional relationships. Building and maintaining strong relationships is critical for career progression and job satisfaction. Yet, the Monday blues can lead to missed opportunities for networking, mentorship, and collaboration, as individuals are more insular and less inclined to reach out.

Decision-making abilities are compromised. When we're not at our best mentally and emotionally, the quality of decisions made can suffer. This can lead to poor judgment calls that affect not only the individual's projects but can also have wider implications for their team or organization.

Last but not least, personal development and career progression suffer. Opportunities for training, taking on new responsibilities, or leading projects are less likely to be pursued with vigor by someone battling the Monday blues. This stagnation affects not only the individual's growth but also the innovation and adaptability of their employing organization.

In summary, the reach of Monday blues extends far beyond a mere personal inconvenience, permeating various facets of job performance and organizational health. By recognizing and addressing these challenges, we can unlock the full potential of our workdays, transforming Mondays from a weekly hurdle to an opportunity for growth, engagement, and productivity.

Chapter 3:
How to Eliminate Monday Blues

Emerging from the sweet embrace of the weekend into the structured world of Monday can feel less like a transition and more like a harsh awakening. But it doesn't have to be this way. A crucial step in banishing those Monday blues is reimagining how we approach the start of our workweek. One potent strategy is completing those daunting Monday morning tasks on Friday. By doing so, we lift the weight off our shoulders even before the weekend begins. This proactive approach not only clears our mind but also paves the way for a smoother transition into the workweek. It's about setting ourselves up for success, making Monday less of a mountain to climb and more of a gentle hill to stroll up.

Another transformative approach is adjusting how we wrap up and start our week. Establishing a Sunday evening routine that calms the mind and prepares the body for the week ahead can be monumentally beneficial. Whether it's a quiet night of reading, planning your week ahead, or indulging in a self-care activity, the goal is to transition into Monday with ease and grace. Coupled with a compelling Monday morning ritual — be it a vigorous workout, a nourishing breakfast, or a few moments of meditation — we not only enhance our mood but set a positive tone that resonates throughout the week.

Such rituals anchor us, reminding us that we have the power to face the week with vigor and a positive outlook.

It's paramount to remember that combating Monday blues is not just about actions, but also mindset. Starting the week with positivity, ensuring adequate sleep, and maintaining good nutrition and exercise habits are foundational elements. When we integrate these into our lives, we're not just tackling Monday; we're transforming our entire approach to work and well-being. It's about harnessing the energy of a new week as an opportunity to thrive, to reconnect with our purpose, and to remember that joy in our work and lives is not just a possibility but a choice. Monday then becomes not a day to dread but a canvas on which to paint a week of accomplishment and fulfillment.

Completing Monday Morning Tasks on Friday

There's a secret weapon that remarkably shifts how we perceive and tackle the infamous Monday blues. It's a strategy as simple as it is effective: completing Monday's tasks on Friday. This concept leverages the power of preparation and foresight to transform the start of your workweek from a daunting challenge into an opportunity for ease and productivity.

Imagine approaching the end of your Friday with a sense of anticipation rather than dread for the upcoming week. This shift in mindset stems from the empowering practice of looking ahead and addressing Monday's to-dos before you switch off your work mode for the weekend. In essence, it's about reclaiming your Mondays, ensuring they're no longer a source of stress but a continuation of your productivity.

Why does this simple shift have such a profound impact? It alleviates the cognitive load that tends to accumulate over the weekend. Knowing that Monday's tasks have been acknowledged and set into motion allows for a more relaxed, enjoyable weekend. You're not just resting your body but easing your mind, too.

There's also the undeniable benefits of a head start. Walking into work on Monday with tasks already underway provides an immediate sense of accomplishment and momentum. It's akin to starting a race several strides ahead — psychologically, you're primed for success.

Moreover, this practice promotes a deeper, more strategic engagement with your work. By planning and acting on Monday's tasks beforehand, you're essentially forecasting potential challenges and opportunities. This strategic foresight often leads to improved decision-making and prioritization, qualities that enhance job performance across the board.

Implementing this shift does require discipline and a proactive mindset. As Friday afternoon rolls around, there's a natural temptation to wind down, to push unfinished tasks onto future you. However, this is where a change in perspective is crucial. Consider this time as an investment in your future well-being, a deposit into your own peace of mind.

To start, identify tasks that can realistically be tackled or at least prepared on Friday. This doesn't mean you need to complete every task in its entirety but setting the stage for Monday's work can make a substantial difference. Whether it's drafting emails, organizing your workspace, or simply jotting down a plan of action. Every little bit counts.

It's also helpful to categorize tasks by their urgency and importance. Not all tasks are created equal, and recognizing which tasks will have the most significant impact on your week can help prioritize your Friday efforts. By focusing on high-impact tasks, you ensure that your Monday starts on the most productive foot possible.

Communication plays a pivotal role in this strategy. Inform your team of your plans to tackle Monday's tasks ahead of time. This not only sets expectations but can also encourage a culture of efficiency and foresight within your team. Collaboration and shared goals are powerful motivators and can make this transition smoother and more beneficial for everyone involved.

Of course, it's essential to strike a balance. The goal is not to cram all of Monday's work into Friday, creating an overwhelming end to your week. Instead, it's about thoughtful preparation and incremental progress. It's making sure that you set the next week up for success without sacrificing your current well-being.

Admittedly, it takes time to adjust to this approach. Initially, you might struggle with the discipline it requires or the redistribution of your workload. Yet, like any habit, consistency is key. Over time, what once felt like an added effort will become second nature, seamlessly integrated into your end-of-week routine.

This strategy isn't just about boosting productivity; it's equally about enhancing your work-life balance. By minimizing Monday's pressures, you foster a smoother transition from weekend to workweek, reducing the dread that can often overshadow Sunday nights. It's about entering your week feeling prepared, not panicked.

Moreover, beginning Monday's tasks on Friday exemplifies a powerful commitment to self-care in the workplace. It's a practice that respects the need for genuine downtime, acknowledging that rest is not merely the absence of work but a state of reduced mental burden. This commitment to self-care is crucial for sustaining motivation and job satisfaction over the long term.

In conclusion, the practice of beginning Monday's tasks on Friday is a transformative strategy that addresses the Monday blues from a proactive standpoint. It's a testament to the power of preparation, foresight, and the subtle shift in mindset that can redefine the start of our workweek. As you embrace this approach, you'll find that Mondays aren't just manageable; they're an opportunity to excel and enjoy your work from a place of ease and readiness.

Remember, the key to overcoming Monday blues lies not just in facing them head-on but in rearranging our work and mindset to minimize their impact. It's about turning the dreaded Monday into just another day where you can thrive, achieving a harmonious balance between work and life. Through this practice, we can collectively transform our approach to work, making every day, not just Friday, a reason to celebrate progress and productivity.

Considering an Alternative Monday Schedule

As we delve deeper into the art of conquering the Monday Blues, it's essential to tackle one innovative strategy head-on: considering an alternative Monday schedule. This isn't merely about shuffling tasks around; it involves fundamentally rethinking how we approach the first day of the workweek to improve our work-life balance and, ultimately, our job performance.

The traditional Monday-to-Friday, 9-to-5 work schedule is deeply ingrained in the corporate culture. However, it's worth questioning whether this age-old structure serves us well or if it amplifies the dread of Monday mornings. An alternative Monday schedule could be the breath of fresh air needed to revitalize our week's start.

Imagine a Monday where you're not bound by the usual early morning alarm clock, rushing to beat morning traffic. Instead, you have the flexibility to start your day at a time that suits you best, perhaps even from the comfort of your home. This shift can make a monumental difference in transitioning from leisurely weekend vibes to the workweek hustle.

Flexibility on Mondays can also mean a shifted focus on the type of work done. It might involve dedicating the day to planning, creative thinking, or catching up on reading and research rather than diving straight into meetings or high-intensity tasks. This gradual transition can soften the jolt between weekend freedom and weekday obligations.

Adopting a more flexible Monday schedule might also include the concept of a compressed workweek. This could involve working longer hours from Tuesday to Friday to accommodate a shorter day on Monday or even every other Monday off, creating a long weekend effect twice a month. While not feasible for every job or industry, even the smallest strides toward flexibility can significantly impact morale.

While contemplating these alternatives, it's crucial to consider the ripple effects such changes might have. Coordination with your team and clear communication are paramount to ensure productivity doesn't falter. It also means being diligent about not letting the flexibility convert into less work time overall, unless that's the agreed-upon arrangement.

For many of us, the dread of Monday lies not in the day itself but in what it represents: a sudden halt to freedom and relaxation, met with an abrupt return to stress and obligations. An alternative Monday schedule seeks to blur these harsh lines, offering a gentler return to our professional roles.

It's also vital to frame this concept within the context of personal responsibility and self-awareness. What works for one might not suit another. Knowing your peak productivity periods, work preferences, and how you best transition into work mode can guide you in customizing an alternative Monday that suits your needs.

Implementing an alternative Monday schedule requires a paradigm shift at both the individual and organizational levels. It's about recognizing that employee well-being is directly linked to productivity and that rigid schedules can sometimes be more of a hindrance than a help.

Encouraging this change might also necessitate a reevaluation of how we measure productivity and success. Moving away from the quantity of hours to the quality of output can foster a more fulfilling and balanced work life, while also diminishing the Monday dread.

From an HR perspective, introducing flexible Monday schedules could be a game-changer in terms of recruitment and retention. In today's job market, where work-life balance is increasingly prioritized, this could give companies a competitive edge in attracting top talent.

For those in leadership roles, modeling and advocating for flexibility can create a culture shift within the organization. It sends a powerful message that employee well-being is valued and that the company is willing to innovate for its workforce's benefit.

Of course, exploring an alternative Monday schedule isn't without its challenges. It demands a level of introspection, adaptability, and commitment from both employers and employees. However, the potential benefits in employee satisfaction, productivity, and overall work-life harmony make it a pursuit worth considering.

As we reflect on the possibilities of redefining the start of our workweek, it's clear that embracing flexibility could play a crucial role in eliminating the Monday Blues. It's about creating a work environment that acknowledges and adapts to the human element, understanding that a more satisfied and well-balanced workforce is the cornerstone of success.

In conclusion, considering an alternative Monday schedule could be a transformative step towards reshaping our work lives. It challenges the status quo, offering a fresh perspective on work-life balance and opening the door to a more motivated, energized, and engaged workforce. As we continue to navigate the complexities of work-life dynamics, such innovations may very well hold the key to unlocking a happier, more productive Monday experience.

Avoid Over-scheduling

As we pivot from understanding the foundational concerns behind Monday Blues to actionable strategies, it becomes imperative to highlight a critical but often overlooked aspect: avoiding over-scheduling. The allure of maximizing productivity can lead one into a trap of cramming too much into the limited hours of a day, especially as one transitions from the freedom of the weekend into the structured reality of the workweek.

The phenomenon of over-scheduling oneself, especially on a Monday, stems from a variety of intentions. Sometimes it's the eagerness to catch up, other times it's the pressure to prove one's dedication. However, this overzealous approach often backfires, leaving one feeling drained, unfocused, and even less productive than if a more measured pace had been adopted. The key is striking a balance: ensuring that you're productive without overburdening yourself right out of the gate.

To evade the pitfall of over-scheduling, it's crucial to start with realistic expectations of what can be accomplished. Reflecting on your most productive days can offer insights into how much you can realistically achieve without setting yourself up for failure. Remember, quality is better than quantity; it's not about how many tasks you can cram into a day but how effectively you can accomplish them.

Moreover, prioritization becomes a tool of unparalleled importance in the quest to avoid over-scheduling. Identifying the tasks that need your immediate attention versus those that can wait plays a crucial part in managing your workload. Embrace the art of saying 'no' or 'later' to tasks that don't serve your immediate goals, thereby freeing up space to focus on what truly matters.

An unexpected ally in avoiding over-scheduling is the establishment of boundaries, particularly with regard to work. In an age where technology blurs the lines between work and home, setting clear boundaries ensures that your work doesn't encroach upon your personal time. This is especially vital on Mondays when the transition from weekend to work mode needs to be as smooth as possible to mitigate the Monday Blues.

Implementing time management tools and techniques can also offer significant relief from over-scheduling. Whether it's a digital app that blocks off your schedule or a physical planner that lays out your week, finding a system that works for you is key. This helps in creating a visual representation of your time and assists in identifying when you're overloading your day.

Transition times between tasks are often overlooked yet are essential in preventing over-scheduling. Allotting buffer time between commitments can provide a much-needed mental break, decreasing stress and increasing overall productivity. It's these small pauses that allow you to catch your breath and prepare for what's next, making each task more manageable.

A mindset shift is also in order when tackling the problem of over-scheduling. Viewing time as a finite resource that needs to be invested wisely shifts one's approach from trying to do everything to focusing on accomplishing what aligns with your goals and well-being. This mindset not only helps in reducing over-scheduling but also enhances satisfaction in the tasks you do complete.

Listening to your body and acknowledging your limits is also a critical step. Over-scheduling often leads to burnout, and the signs of approaching burnout can be subtle. Recognizing when you're stretching yourself too thin and allowing yourself to step back and reevaluate your commitments is necessary for long-term productivity and health.

Empowering yourself to delegate tasks is another strategy that combats over-scheduling. Whether at work or in personal commitments, understanding that you don't have to tackle everything alone can vastly reduce your workload. By sharing responsibilities, you not only ease your own schedule but also foster teamwork and collaboration.

Finally, acknowledging that perfection is an illusion will aid immensely. The pursuit of perfection often leads to adding unnecessary tasks or redoing work, which in turn contributes to over-scheduling. Embrace a mindset of excellence instead, where doing your best within set limitations is the goal. This approach is not only realistic but also rewarding.

Incorporating these strategies into your approach to scheduling, especially as you plan for Mondays, can significantly alleviate the dread that comes with the start of the week. By avoiding over-scheduling, you allow yourself the space to breathe, focus, and excel in your tasks, setting a positive and productive tone for the week ahead.

Initiating your week with a balanced schedule not only combats the Monday Blues but also sets a precedent for healthy work habits. It's about giving yourself the permission to step into your week with grace rather than sprinting into it with urgency.

Remember, the objective is to start your week feeling empowered and in control, rather than overwhelmed and frazzled. Embracing these strategies will not only improve your Mondays but will also contribute to a more balanced work-life harmony, enhancing both your job performance and your overall well-being.

Taking a moment to reflect on and adjust your scheduling habits can have profound effects not only on your Mondays but on your entire workweek. Begin with being mindful of your tendency to over-schedule and gradually integrate these practices into your routine. The transformation you'll experience in your work and personal life will be tangible, turning dreaded Mondays into opportunities for growth and productivity.

Establish a Sunday Evening Routine

As we delve into the strategies for conquering the notorious Monday Blues, it's essential to address the power of establishing a Sunday evening routine. This routine isn't just about planning; it's a ritual that sets the tone for the entire week, transforming dread into anticipation, and fear into empowerment. The following paragraphs outline a strategic approach to creating a Sunday routine that not only eases the transition into Monday but also enriches your overall work-life balance and job performance.

The cornerstone of any successful Sunday routine starts with reflection. Taking a moment to sit back and reflect on the past week can help you appreciate your accomplishments, learn from your setbacks, and reset your focus for the week ahead. This practice isn't about dwelling on the negatives but rather about acknowledging them, understanding them, and then moving forward with clarity and purpose.

Preparation plays a crucial role in this routine. This isn't about cramming in all the tasks you've been procrastinating on over the weekend. Instead, it's about thoughtful organization and prioritization. Look at your calendar for the upcoming week, identify key tasks and meetings, and set realistic goals for what you want to achieve. This approach not only helps reduce anxiety but also allows for a more focused and productive week.

Detachment is another critical aspect of your Sunday evening routine. It's vital to consciously disconnect from work-related communications. This means setting boundaries around checking emails or work messages. Such a practice helps in creating a mental space where work doesn't consume every moment of your life, allowing you to fully recharge and engage with personal activities or family time.

Self-care should be non-negotiable in your Sunday routine. Whether it's reading, taking a long bath, practicing yoga, or engaging in any activity that brings you joy and relaxation, make it a priority. These activities not only help in reducing stress but also in boosting your mood and energy levels, readying you for the week ahead.

Meal preparation can also be a game-changer. Preparing meals for the week or even just for Monday can alleviate the rush and stress of having to cook amidst a busy schedule. It's about nourishing your body with healthy choices that fuel your energy and concentration levels, making you more capable of facing the challenges of the new week.

Sleep is, without a doubt, a crucial element of your Sunday routine. Ensuring you get a good night's sleep on Sunday sets the stage for a week of productivity and focus. It's worth adjusting your Sunday activities to ensure you can wind down in time and enjoy a restful, uninterrupted night of sleep.

Visualization and setting intentions for the week can also significantly influence your mindset. Spend a few quiet moments envisioning your week, the tasks you aim to complete, and how you want to feel. Pairing this visualization with positive affirmations can help shift your outlook from dread to opportunity.

For those who struggle with the abrupt transition into Monday, consider a 'soft start' to your week. This could be a ritual you look forward to, like a special breakfast, a music playlist that lifts your spirits, or an early morning walk. Incorporating something you love into your Monday routine can make the start of the workweek something to anticipate.

Moreover, limit to-do lists for Monday to a few critical tasks. Overloading your Monday with back-to-back tasks is a surefire way to fuel anxiety and stress. By setting a lighter, more manageable schedule, you allow yourself to ease into the week without feeling overwhelmed from the get-go.

Stay flexible. While having a routine is beneficial, rigidity can lead to stress when things don't go as planned. Approach your Sunday evening routine with a mindset of flexibility, adapting as necessary to meet your needs and circumstances.

Engage with your support system, whether that's family or friends. Discussing your plans for the week or even some of the challenges you anticipate can provide a sense of shared experience and support, making the week ahead seem less daunting.

Emphasize gratitude by jotting down a few things you're thankful for from the past week. This practice can significantly alter your perspective, shifting focus from anxiety about the week ahead to appreciation of the present moment.

Remember that this routine is personal to you. What works for someone else might not necessarily fit your lifestyle or preferences. The key is to develop a Sunday evening ritual that resonates with you, aligning with your goals, values, and needs.

Establishing a Sunday evening routine is a profound step towards mitigating the Monday Blues. It's about preparation, reflection, self-care, and setting the right intentions. By creating a routine that fosters a positive transition into the workweek, you not only enhance your job performance and work-life balance but also transform the way you perceive Mondays—from a day of dread to a day of opportunity.

Establishing a Monday Morning Ritual

In the quest to conquer the Monday blues, establishing a Monday morning ritual is akin to laying down the first stone on a path to a more harmonious work-life balance. Think of it as setting the tone for your entire week. This section dives into creating a ritual that not only combats the dread of Mondays but also enhances your overall job performance and satisfaction.

First and foremost, understand that a ritual is more than just a routine. It's an intentional practice imbued with meaning and purpose. Your Monday morning doesn't have to start with the blaring of an alarm followed by the mechanical motions of getting ready for work. Instead, it can begin with a series of carefully chosen actions that ground you and prepare you for the week ahead.

Consider waking up a bit earlier than usual. This extra time is not to start working right off the bat, but to allow yourself a moment of solitude and quietness. In these early hours, the world is still waking up, and there's a unique kind of peace that can help set a positive tone for your day.

A key component of your Monday ritual should involve some form of mindfulness or meditation. Even just a few minutes of deep breathing, mindfulness meditation, or gentle yoga can significantly reduce stress and anxiety levels, clearing your mind and enhancing your focus for the day ahead.

Nourishment plays a crucial role in how we feel, both physically and mentally. Incorporate a nutritious and enjoyable breakfast into your morning ritual. Eating a meal that is both satisfying and healthy can provide you with the energy you need to face the day.

Journaling is another powerful tool that can be integrated into your Monday morning ritual. Take a moment to jot down your thoughts, intentions, or goals for the week. This practice not only helps in organizing your thoughts but also in setting a clear direction for the week.

Visualizing your day can also make a significant difference. Spend a few minutes imagining your day going smoothly, accomplishing your tasks, and overcoming challenges with ease. This mental rehearsal prepares you for success and boosts your confidence.

Gentle exercise, like a short walk or stretching session, can invigorate your body and awaken your senses. Exercise releases endorphins, the body's natural mood lifters, and helps combat stress and anxiety.

Making your bed and tidying up your living space might seem trivial, but these small acts of cleanliness and organization provide a sense of control and achievement, which can be incredibly empowering.

Choose your outfit the night before to eliminate one decision from your Monday morning. This not only saves time but also reduces decision fatigue, allowing your mental energy to be focused on more important tasks.

Before starting your work, take a moment to connect with something that inspires you. It could be reading a few pages from a motivational book, listening to an uplifting playlist, or simply stepping outside to appreciate nature. This connection can provide a much-needed boost of inspiration.

Throughout your morning, maintain an attitude of gratitude. Mentally list three things you're grateful for. Gratitude shifts your focus from what you feel you lack to the abundance that is already present in your life, fostering a positive mindset.

Finally, transition to your work responsibilities gradually. Start with a task you enjoy or one that's easier to manage. This sets a positive momentum for the rest of the day and makes the more challenging tasks seem less daunting.

Creating and maintaining a Monday morning ritual is not about filling every moment with activity. It's about choosing actions that bring you joy, peace, and energy. It's about starting your week off on the right foot, armed with optimism and preparedness.

Remember, the ritual you establish is uniquely yours. What works for one person may not work for another. The key is to experiment until you find the sequence that feels right for you. By crafting a Monday morning that you actually look forward to, you're not only setting the stage for a productive week but also cultivating a life that feels more balanced and fulfilling.

Starting Your Week with Positivity

Kicking off your week on the right foot isn't just about avoiding the notorious Monday blues; it's about setting a tone that will carry you through the week with energy, productivity, and, most importantly, positivity. Embracing a positive mindset from the moment your alarm buzzes on Monday morning can transform your entire week. But how, you might wonder, can one shift from dread to anticipation, from survival mode to thriving? The secret lies in intentionality, ritual, and a bit of strategic planning.

First and foremost, understanding that your mindset plays a colossal role in how you perceive and tackle your week is crucial. A mindset entrenched in negativity and apprehension creates a self-fulfilling prophecy of stress and dissatisfaction. However, approaching the week with optimism and openness to opportunities can significantly alter your experience for the better. This doesn't mean ignoring the challenges ahead but rather choosing to focus on what you can control—your attitude and reactions.

Creating a Sunday routine that emphasizes relaxation and preparation can ease the transition into Monday. Instead of cramming in last-minute chores or work tasks, dedicate Sunday evening to calming activities that bring you joy and relaxation. Whether it's reading, a leisurely walk, or a family dinner, these activities can help mitigate the shock of the upcoming work-week, mentally preparing you for a fresh start.

Visualizing your week ahead on Sunday can also be a powerful tool. Spend a few quiet moments thinking about what you wish to achieve and how you want to feel throughout the week. Visualization is a great method to align your subconscious with your conscious goals, making you more likely to navigate your week with purpose and positivity.

Incorporating a Monday morning ritual that you genuinely look forward to can drastically improve your disposition towards the day. Maybe it's a special kind of coffee, a favorite playlist, or a brief morning walk. Whatever it is, let it be something that excites you to get up and start your day. This ritual acts as a bridge between the comfort of the weekend and the productivity of the week, making Monday mornings something to anticipate, not dread.

Gratitude is another powerful tool to wield against the Monday blues. Starting your week by jotting down three things you're grateful for can shift your perspective from focusing on what you 'have to do' to what you 'get to do'. This subtle shift in language and perspective is incredibly effective in cultivating a mindset of abundance and opportunity.

Acknowledging that sluggish feelings on Monday are normal can also alleviate the pressure to be instantly on top form. Recognize that your body and mind may need a little extra time to gear up after the weekend. Allowing yourself grace and space to slowly ramp up your productivity can prevent feelings of frustration and inadequacy.

Setting small, achievable goals for Monday can also create momentum for the rest of the week. Instead of overwhelming yourself with the week's most challenging tasks, choose lighter, more manageable tasks that you can confidently accomplish.

This sense of achievement early in the week can boost your confidence and motivation for more significant challenges ahead.

Connect with coworkers or friends who inspire positivity in you. Sharing your intentions for a positive week and discussing what you're looking forward to can help reinforce your own mindset and potentially lift theirs. Positivity, after all, is contagious.

Remember, starting your week with positivity is a choice and a practice. It's about making deliberate decisions that uplift and inspire you, recognizing that every Monday offers a new opportunity for growth and joy. Rather than mourning the end of the weekend, embrace the beginning of a new, potentially wonderful week.

Prepare your work and living spaces to reflect the positivity you wish to embody. A clean, organized environment can significantly affect your mental clarity and emotional state. Taking time on Sunday to tidy up and prepare your workspace can make the Monday morning start much smoother and more pleasant.

Reframe challenges as opportunities for growth. As you look at the week ahead, adopting a growth mindset toward tasks or situations that may seem daunting can transform them into experiences from which you can learn and evolve. This approach not only fosters positivity but also resilience.

Hydrate and nourish your body with food that makes you feel good. It's not uncommon to indulge over the weekend, but come Monday, focusing on hydrating and eating nutritious foods can significantly impact your energy levels and mood. Treat your body kindly, and it will support you through the week.

Be patient with yourself. The journey to embracing Monday and starting your week with a burst of positivity is a process. Some weeks will be easier than others, and that's okay. What's important is that you're making an effort to change your perspective, which is a significant step in itself.

Banishing the Monday blues and beginning your week with a burst of positivity is entirely within your reach. It involves a combination of mindset shifts, purposeful routines, and a commitment to self-care and preparation. By implementing these strategies, you're not just improving your Mondays; you're setting the stage for a happier, more fulfilling life.

Ensuring Adequate Sleep

One of the cornerstone habits that can significantly help in eliminating Monday morning blues is ensuring a pattern of adequate sleep. It's an irrefutable fact that the quality of our sleep directly impacts our mood, energy levels, and ability to focus—all essential factors for starting the week strong. When Sunday night rolls around, it's crucial to prioritize a sleeping environment and routine that encourages restful sleep.

First, let's address the importance of consistency. Just as we benefit from regular eating and exercise schedules, our bodies thrive on consistent sleep patterns. Going to bed and waking up at the same time every day, including weekends, helps regulate our body's internal clock and improves the quality of our sleep. While it might be tempting to stay up late and sleep in on the weekends, this can disrupt our sleep pattern and make Mondays feel even more challenging.

Creating a tranquil sleep environment is also key. This means paying attention to factors such as temperature, noise, and light. Most experts agree that a cool, dark, and quiet bedroom promotes better sleep. Consider investing in blackout curtains, earplugs, or a white noise machine if necessary. In addition, the comfort of your mattress and pillows should not be overlooked as they play a vital role in supporting a good night's sleep.

Engaging in a relaxing pre-sleep routine can signal to your body that it's time to wind down. This could include activities like reading, taking a warm bath, or practicing gentle yoga or meditation. Avoiding stimulating activities such as screen time from phones, tablets, and computers is crucial since the blue light emitted can interfere with our natural sleep cycle.

Caffeine and heavy meals late in the day can be obstacles to a restful night. Try to limit caffeine consumption after lunch and aim to have dinner at least a few hours before bedtime. If hunger strikes later, opt for a light snack rather than a full meal to prevent sleep disruptions.

Exercise is another powerful tool for combating sleep issues. Regular physical activity can help you fall asleep faster and enjoy deeper sleep. However, timing is important—try to finish exercising at least a few hours before bedtime so that your body has time to cool down and relax.

The role of stress in affecting our sleep cannot be understated. Developing strategies for managing stress, such as mindfulness or deep-breathing exercises, can make a significant difference in our ability to relax and drift off to sleep. Recognizing and addressing worries or anxieties well before bedtime ensures they're less likely to keep you up at night.

For those times when sleep seems elusive despite your best efforts, it's helpful to have a strategy in place. Lying in bed tossing and turning can reinforce negative associations with the bedroom environment. Instead, get up and engage in a quiet, non-stimulative activity until you feel sleepy.

It's also vital to examine your daytime nap habits. While short power naps can be beneficial, especially for making up for lost sleep, long or late-in-the-day naps can hinder nighttime sleep quality. If you choose to nap, aim to keep it early in the day and under 30 minutes.

Underlying health conditions, such as sleep disorders, can significantly impact our sleep quality. If you suspect that an underlying health issue might be affecting your sleep, it's important to consult a healthcare provider. Addressing these issues can lead to marked improvements in sleep quality and, consequently, in how you face Mondays.

Acknowledging the tie between alcohol consumption and sleep is crucial. While alcohol might seem like it helps you fall asleep faster, it actually disrupts the sleep cycle, leading to poorer quality sleep. Limiting alcohol intake, especially in the hours leading up to bedtime, can help improve sleep quality.

Incorporating mindfulness and relaxation techniques into your evening routine can also prepare your mind for rest. Techniques like progressive muscle relaxation or guided imagery can ease the transition into sleep by reducing physical tension and mental stress.

Understanding the impact of our sleep environment extends to electronic devices not just because of the blue light. The mental stimulation from consuming content or engaging in social media can make it harder for our brains to shift into sleep mode. Keeping electronic devices out of the bedroom—or setting a strict cutoff time—can help mitigate this.

The value of a positive mindset about sleep and the forthcoming week cannot be overstated. Reframing thoughts about Mondays from dread to optimism can reduce Sunday night anxiety and contribute to better sleep. Visualizing a successful week ahead and setting intentions can make the transition into Monday not only smoother but something to look forward to.

Through these strategies, you can transform your sleep into a powerful ally against the Monday blues. Adequate sleep sets a positive domino effect into motion, enhancing not only our work-life balance and job performance but our overall quality of life. By reclaiming our nights, we reclaim our days—and it all starts with conquering Sunday night sleep.

Understanding How Diet Affects Monday Mornings

The journey to overcoming the Monday blues is multifaceted, touching on aspects of our lives that we may not regularly connect to our mood or performance at the start of the week. Among these, the role of diet proves to be significantly influential, serving not just as fuel but as a mood modulator that can either set us up for success or contribute to stagnant Mondays.

It's common knowledge that the foods we consume play a crucial role in our physical health. However, the connection between diet and mental well-being is often underestimated. Emerging research suggests that the food choices we make over the weekend can profoundly impact how we feel and perform on Monday morning. The bridge between Sunday's dinner and Monday's mood is built on biochemistry, with nutrients affecting neurotransmitter pathways and hormonal balances that influence our state of mind.

Let's start with a simple yet powerful premise: high-quality fuels lead to high-quality performance. Just as a luxury car runs best on premium gasoline, our bodies and minds operate at their best when nourished with nutrient-dense foods. The pleasure of indulging in comfort food or experiencing a sugar high often comes with a hidden cost, manifesting as lethargy, irritability, or a foggy mind come Monday. These symptoms can exacerbate the usual Monday blues, making it even harder to find motivation and positivity.

Furthermore, the concept of the "gut-brain axis" highlights how our digestive system's health directly impacts our mental state. The gastrointestinal tract is teeming with billions of bacteria that play a role in producing and regulating key neurotransmitters like serotonin, often referred to as the happiness hormone. A weekend of heavy, processed foods may disrupt this delicate balance, leading to feelings of anxiety or a downturn in mood at the start of the week.

Hydration is yet another critical factor that is easily overlooked. Adequate water intake is essential for all our bodily functions, including cognition and mood regulation. Starting

Monday morning in a state of dehydration, perhaps after a weekend of not paying attention to fluid intake, can make the blues feel even bluer. We face an uphill battle against fatigue, impaired focus, and a more pronounced feeling of stress.

So, how can we harness the power of nutrition to combat the Monday blues? A starting point is being mindful of our dietary choices, especially during the weekend. Opting for meals rich in vegetables, fruits, lean proteins, and whole grains can bolster our mood and energy levels, setting a positive tone for the week ahead.

Incorporating foods that are high in omega-3 fatty acids, such as salmon, walnuts, and flaxseeds, can also play a part in lifting our spirits. These essential fats are known for their anti-inflammatory properties and potential to lessen symptoms of depression and anxiety.

Planning meals ahead can make a pivotal difference. By preparing balanced, nutritious options for Sunday dinner or for meals throughout Monday, we give ourselves a clear path to follow, eliminating the stress of meal decisions in the midst of the Monday rush.

Equally important is paying attention to what we drink. Choosing water or herbal teas over sugary or alcoholic beverages can prevent the swings in blood sugar levels and mood that often accompany less healthy choices. A mindful approach to consumption sets a stable foundation for the week.

A snack strategy can also be a game-changer. Having nutrient-rich snacks on hand, such as nuts, yogurt, or fresh fruit, helps maintain stable energy levels and supports a positive mood throughout the day, combating the common mid-morning or mid-afternoon slumps.

But it's not just about what we eat. When we eat plays a role too. Maintaining regular meal times, even on weekends, helps regulate our body's internal clock. This consistency aids in smoother transitions between days of the week, reducing the shock to our system that a drastic shift in routine can cause.

Modifying our diet to support our mental well-being is not about strict restrictions or denying ourselves the joy of food. Rather, it's about making conscious choices that enhance our mood and energy levels, empowering us to face Mondays with renewed vigor and enthusiasm.

In times of stress or when the Monday blues hit harder than usual, it's tempting to reach for comfort foods that offer a temporary emotional lift. While there's room for moderation and occasional treats, recognizing and resisting these impulses can be a powerful step in mastering our moods and welcoming Mondays with open arms.

Finally, remember that transformation doesn't happen overnight. Gradual changes, sustained over time, can lead to lasting benefits. A weekend indulgence isn't a defeat; it's a re-minder of the balance we strive to achieve. Each meal is a new opportunity to support our mental health and improve our outlook on the days ahead.

In essence, the battle against the Monday blues is fought on many fronts, with diet playing the role of both shield and sword. By being proactive about our food and drink choices, we arm ourselves with the tools needed to transform how we experience the start of the week, turning what was once a time of dread into a period of potential and positivity.

Understanding How Exercise Affects Mood and Energy

Embarking on the journey to mitigate the Monday blues, it's imperative we explore how regular physical activity intertwines with our emotional and energy landscapes. The connection between exercise and mood elevation is not just anecdotal; it's steeped in scientific evidence, offering a beacon of hope for transforming our Mondays from dreaded to anticipated.

At a glance, the act of exercising stimulates various brain chemicals that might leave you feeling happier and more relaxed. This biochemical process includes the release of endorphins, often referred to as the body's feel-good neurotransmitters. These naturally occurring chemicals play a critical role in managing our perception of pain and can usher in a euphoric sensation sometimes coined as the "runner's high."

Moreover, engaging in physical activities can enhance our overall well-being by improving quality of sleep. It's well-documented that exercising helps regulate our sleep patterns, a fundamental component of combating fatigue and boosting energy levels. Adequate sleep is paramount, especially when addressing the lethargy that often accompanies the start of a new workweek.

Another dimension to consider is the impact of exercise on self-esteem and cognitive function. Regular physical activity can be a powerful tool in building self-esteem, improving memory, and sharpening judgment skills, even under stress.

This, in essence, creates a fortified mental reservoir that can be tapped into when navigating challenges, including the anticipatory anxiety of Mondays.

The relationship between physical activity and stress reduction cannot be overstated. Exercise acts as a stress buffer by increasing concentrations of norepinephrine, a chemical that can moderate the brain's response to stress. Thus, by incorporating regular physical activity into our routine, we can develop a more resilient stress response system, making us less susceptible to the overwhelming wave of Monday blues.

Choosing the right type of exercise can also play a crucial role in how we experience its mood-lifting benefits. Whether it's a brisk walk, a cycling class, or a yoga session, the key is to find activities that are enjoyable and sustainable in the long term. The enjoyment factor significantly contributes to the consistency of exercise, which is vital for reaping its long-lasting mood and energy enhancements.

It's essential to approach exercise with a mindset that embraces gradual progression rather than immediate perfection. Starting with small, achievable goals can help build the foundation for a lasting habit. This incremental approach ensures that exercise remains a source of joy and empowerment rather than becoming another daunting task on our to-do list.

Furthermore, the social aspect of exercising, whether joining a class, a club, or simply engaging in activities with friends or family, can amplify its mood-boosting effects. Social support and connection play a critical role in mental health, and combining these elements with physical activity can lead to a more enriched and balanced life.

Understanding that motivation can be a significant barrier, especially after a relaxing weekend, finding ways to integrate exercise into our Monday routine can offer a promising start. Perhaps it's a morning stretching routine, a post-lunch walk, or an evening dance class. The idea is to build anticipation and a sense of achievement that counterbalances the Monday blues.

Consistency is the golden thread that ties together the mood and energy benefits of exercise. It's not just about a one-time effort but embedding physical activity into our daily lives as a non-negotiable component of our wellness strategy. This habitual practice can gradually shift our experience of Mondays from something we endure to something we can genuinely look forward to.

Let's not overlook the role of diet in conjunction with exercise. A balanced diet can further enhance the mood and energy benefits of physical activity. Together, they form a powerful duo in bolstering our resilience against stress and fatigue, especially pertinent at the start of the workweek.

Tapping into the transformative power of exercise requires a holistic view that acknowledges its multifaceted benefits for our physical, emotional, and cognitive well-being. As we embark on this journey, let's remind ourselves that the path to overcoming the Monday blues is not just about changing one aspect of our lives but adopting a comprehensive approach that nurtures our body, mind, and spirit.

Embracing exercise as a cornerstone of this strategy offers a hopeful perspective for reimagining our Mondays. It's not merely about enduring the start of the week but thriving in it, fueled by the heightened mood, enhanced focus, and replenished energy that regular physical activity provides. By integrating exercise into our lives, we unlock the door to a world where Mondays are no longer a source of dread but an opportunity for renewal and growth.

So, let's step into this new week with a renewed commitment to physical activity, allowing it to light our path toward not just surviving but thriving in every aspect of our work and personal lives. The journey to overcome Monday blues begins with a single step — a step that harnesses the boundless energy and positive mood brought forth by the simple act of moving our bodies.

Improving Motivation

As we delve into the core strategies for defeating Monday blues, we must focus on the backbone of productivity and fulfillment: motivation. Nurturing motivation can transform the start of your workweek from a drudgery into a springboard for success. Finding the drive to power through the early hours of Monday begins with clarifying your goals and aligning them with your actions.

You can't expect to feel fired up if your goals are vague or if your tasks seem inconsequential. Specify what you're aiming for in the short term and how that contributes to your bigger picture. Sometimes, reconnecting with why you chose your job in the first place can reignite the passion that the weekend may have dimmed.

Consider the thrill of a well-earned success. Setting milestones for your Monday can craft a pattern of achievement that fuels further productivity. Break your tasks into digestible segments and celebrate each victory, no matter how small. This tactic doesn't just ease the workload; it builds a framework of consistent reinforcement.

Positivity isn't just a frame of mind; it's a habit that can be cultivated. Start your week by identifying things you're grateful for in your work life. This could be supportive colleagues, a recent achievement, or even the opportunity to learn and grow. Gratitude is a potent motivator and can reframe your approach to Mondays.

Visualizing success is a powerful tool. Spend time envisioning a triumphant Monday. By mentally rehearsing your wins, you condition your mind to expect success, which naturally promotes a more motivated approach to your tasks. This visualization technique prepares you for the challenges ahead and fills you with the confidence to tackle them.

Motivation and physical well-being are deeply linked. Ensure you're fueling your body with the right nutrients and staying hydrated. The food you consume can either be an ally in improving your motivation or an adversary that saps your energy and focus.

Similarly, exercise shouldn't be overlooked. Physical activity triggers endorphins, which act as natural mood boosters. Incorporating a workout into your Monday routine can set a positive tone for the week and furnish you with the zest to conquer your tasks.

Learn to recognize and dismantle procrastination. Procrastination is often rooted in fear—of failure, of the unknown, or of not being good enough. Reframe these fears as opportunities to grow and challenge yourself. Adopting an 'I get to' rather than an 'I have to' mindset is a simple yet effective way to shift your perspective and supercharge your motivation.

Incentivizing your day can also play a critical role in melting away the Monday blues. If there's a particular task you're dreading, pair it with a reward for its completion. This could be a special lunch, a coffee break, or even time spent on a personal project once you've tackled your work responsibilities.

Don't underestimate the power of social connections at your workplace. Engaging with colleagues can provide a boost of encouragement. Share your aims for the day and ask about theirs. Not only does this create a supportive environment, but it also holds you accountable for your stated intentions.

Savvy task management is key. Prioritize your work in a way that aligns with your peak productive hours. For many, the morning brings a fresh burst of energy; use this time to tackle the most challenging or high-priority tasks. This approach ensures that you're leveraging your motivation when it's at its strongest.

Consider the influence of your workspace. A cluttered desk can equate to a cluttered mind. Taking a few minutes to organize your work area can drastically improve your mental clarity and motivation. Personalize your space with items that inspire you and serve as visual motivators, such as pictures of loved ones, goal charts, or motivational quotes.

Don't overlook the psychological impact of attire. Dressing the part can mentally prepare you to dive into your workweek. Choose outfits that make you feel confident and professional. The adage 'dress for the job you want, not the job you have' can inspire a more ambitious mindset.

Give yourself permission to step away when needed. Short, strategic breaks can replenish your motivation. These moments away from your desk are not lost time; they're critical intervals for mental rejuvenation. Use them to take a quick walk, meditate, or engage in deep breathing exercises.

Improving motivation isn't a one-off effort; it's a multifaceted, consistent practice. By addressing the psychological, physical, and environmental factors that contribute to your drive, you can effectively eradicate Monday blues. Embrace each new week with the tenacity to grow, the resilience to overcome challenges, and the passion to achieve your goals.

Enhancing Focus and Concentration

Embarking on the journey to eliminate Monday Blues inevitably brings us to the pivotal topic of enhancing focus and concentration. It's a crucial aspect that not only helps you navigate through Monday with more ease but also elevates your overall job performance and satisfaction. The key lies in understanding the factors that influence our mental clarity and adopting practices that foster a conducive environment for our minds to thrive.

First and foremost, recognizing that our environment plays a significant role in our ability to focus cannot be overstated. A cluttered workspace can reflect and contribute to a cluttered mind. Taking the time to organize your physical and digital workspaces can dramatically increase your mental clarity. This simple yet effective step can make a profound difference in how you approach your work on Monday and beyond.

Another aspect to consider is the power of prioritization. It's easy to feel overwhelmed when faced with a mountain of tasks. However, by identifying the most critical tasks and tackling those first, you can enhance your sense of control and focus. This approach not only helps in managing your workload more effectively but also instills a sense of accomplishment early in the day, which fuels further productivity.

Mindfulness practices have also shown great promise in improving focus and concentration. Techniques such as meditation and controlled breathing exercises can help in centering your mind, reducing stress, and enhancing your ability to focus on the task at hand. Incorporating even a short mindfulness session into your morning routine can set a positive tone for the rest of the day.

Nutrition plays a pivotal role in brain health and its capacity to concentrate. Starting your Monday with a well-balanced meal can provide the necessary fuel your brain needs to operate at its best. Foods rich in omega-3 fatty acids, antioxidants, and vitamins are known to boost cognitive function and thus support better focus throughout the day.

Hydration is another factor that's often overlooked when discussing mental clarity. Even mild dehydration can impair cognitive function and concentration. Ensuring you're adequately hydrated is a simple way to help maintain optimal brain performance.

Exercise is not just beneficial for physical health; it's also a powerful stimulant for mental health. Engaging in a moderate exercise routine can enhance cognitive function, improve mood, and increase energy levels, all of which are critical for maintaining focus and concentration.

Quality sleep is foundational to our ability to focus. A restful Sunday night sets the stage for a productive Monday. Establishing a consistent sleep schedule that ensures you're well-rested is pivotal. Sleep deprivation significantly impacts our cognitive functions, including memory, attention, and concentration.

Breaking down work into manageable chunks is an effective strategy to enhance focus. The Pomodoro Technique, for example, uses timed intervals of focused work followed by short breaks. This not only helps prevent burnout but can also improve concentration and productivity.

In today's digital age, managing distractions is more challenging than ever. Limiting exposure to disruptive elements such as social media during work hours can help maintain a steady focus. There are numerous apps designed to help curb digital distractions, allowing you to dedicate your attention to the tasks that matter most.

Goal setting is another powerful tool in your focus-enhancing arsenal. Setting clear, attainable goals for your day or week provides direction and a roadmap to follow, which can significantly improve your ability to stay focused on your priorities.

Finally, practicing gratitude can surprisingly enhance focus and concentration. By regularly acknowledging what you're thankful for, you cultivate a positive mindset that bolsters resilience against stress and fosters mental clarity.

Transitioning your mindset to view Mondays as an opportunity rather than a hurdle can also make a tremendous difference. Embracing Monday with a positive outlook can motivate you to tackle your tasks with energy and focus.

Remember, enhancing focus and concentration is a dynamic process that involves a combination of strategies tailored to your individual needs and lifestyle. Experimenting with different approaches and consistently applying what works best for you is key to overcoming Monday Blues and achieving greater work-life harmony and job satisfaction.

As we journey through these strategies, it's important to remind ourselves that the pursuit of enhanced focus and concentration is not just about combating Monday Blues. It's about cultivating practices that support our overall well-being and success in every aspect of our lives. With dedication and perseverance, we can transform our experiences of Mondays and set a positive tone for the week ahead.

Addressing Monday Blues with Anxiety and Depression

For many, the dread of Monday isn't merely about transitioning from the freedom of the weekend to the structure of work or school. It extends deeper, intertwining with threads of anxiety and depression that can tighten around one's well-being, making the start of the week even more challenging. Recognizing the unique hurdles those with anxiety and depression face on Mondays is crucial in our journey to reclaim the joy and potential these days hold.

Anxiety and depression can magnify the pressure and stress of Mondays, making tasks and responsibilities feel insurmountable. It's not just about shaking off a case of the Sunday scaries; it's about managing a battle within, where the stakes feel all too real. The first step in overcoming this is acknowledgment. By acknowledging this struggle, we begin to dismantle the stigma and isolation that can accompany mental health challenges, paving the way for support, understanding, and strategies tailored to alleviate the compound effect of Monday blues and mental health.

It's imperative to recognize the cyclical nature of anxiety and depression, especially as they relate to the dread of Mondays. The apprehension starts building on Sunday, sometimes called the "Sunday scaries," which can disrupt sleep patterns. This lack of restorative sleep exacerbates anxiety and depression symptoms, leading to a less resilient mindset to face the week ahead. Understanding this cycle is the first step toward breaking it. Ensuring adequate sleep, thereby, becomes not just advice but a cornerstone strategy for anyone grappling with these challenges.

Grounding techniques can be exceptionally beneficial when anxiety starts to spiral. Simple, mindful breathing exercises can act as an anchor, bringing one's awareness back to the present and away from the mounting dread of the upcoming workweek. Likewise, muscle relaxation techniques can ease the physical tension that anxiety and depression often bring, offering a dual approach to calming both mind and body.

Creating a buffer zone between the weekend and the workweek can also serve as a gentle transition for those particularly sensitive to schedule changes. Establishing a Sunday evening routine that includes activities promoting relaxation and positivity can help. Whether it's a warm bath, reading, or a slow yoga session, the key is in consistency and the intention to soothe anxiety and depression.

For those grappling with depression, starting the week might feel like facing a mountain with no peak in sight. Here, setting small, achievable goals for Monday can create a pathway through the fog. This approach offers tangible proof of progress, combating feelings of worthlessness and boosting self-esteem.

The narrative we tell ourselves about Mondays can also feed into our anxiety and depression. Reframing Mondays from a day of daunting tasks to a day of new beginnings and opportunities can shift our emotional and mental landscapes. Engaging in positive affirmations can reinforce this narrative shift, providing a mental armor against the negativities that anxiety and depression wield.

Maintaining self-care habits is crucial, especially on Mondays. For those battling anxiety and depression, self-care is not indulgent but essential. It's about keeping the foundation strong so the building can withstand the winds. Balanced nutrition, hydration, exercise, and self-compassion are the bricks and mortar of this foundation.

Listening to uplifting music or engaging podcasts during commutes or breaks can also serve as a mood booster. These moments of joy or intellectual engagement can break the cycle of negative thoughts, offering a breather from the inner turmoil.

Journaling is another powerful tool in this context. It can help in externalizing the fears and anxieties that cloud one's mind, making them less daunting. Moreover, writing about the activities or aspects of your job that you're grateful for can shift focus from dread to appreciation, easing the grip of Monday blues.

Importantly, addressing anxiety and depression as factors in the struggle against Monday blues may also involve seeking professional help. Therapists and counselors can offer strategies and support tailored to individual needs, making the mountain of Monday seem more like a manageable hill.

For some, the option of working flexibly or remotely can also alleviate the pressure and stress that compound with anxiety and depression. If possible, discussing these options with employers can open pathways to a more balanced approach to Mondays and the workweek.

Another beneficial practice is scheduling something fun or rewarding for Monday itself. This strategy can help change the narrative about Mondays being only about work and responsibilities, adding a layer of anticipation and positive expectation to the start of the week.

Remembering one's purpose and what they love about their job can also serve as a beacon through the fog of anxiety and depression. This reminder can help shift the focus from the dread of Monday to the contributions and achievements one can accomplish.

While the Monday blues can feel like a daunting hurdle for those with anxiety and depression, a blend of acknowledgment, self-care, reframing strategies, and professional support can illuminate the path to not just surviving but thriving. Mondays, with their unique challenges, also hold unique opportunities for growth, resilience, and joy. Embracing these opportunities starts with the understanding that we are not alone in our struggles, and together, we can find the strength to face the week ahead with hope and positivity.

Breathing Exercises

Navigating the murky waters of Monday blues requires more than just sheer willpower; it's about equipping oneself with practical tools that provide immediate relief and long-term benefits. One such tool, surprisingly simple yet profoundly effective, is the art of breathing exercises. Learning to harness the power of breath can transform not just your Mondays but every day of the week.

Breathing exercises are a cornerstone of stress management. They serve as a bridge, connecting the mind and body, facilitating a state of calm and measured control over one's emotional landscape. When Sunday night rolls around, and the thought of Monday starts to cloud your peace, turning to breathing exercises can offer an instant dose of calm.

Let's start with the basics. Deep breathing, also known as diaphragmatic breathing, is a technique that encourages full oxygen exchange and slows the heartbeat, signaling to the body that it's time to relax. An easy method to begin with is the 4-7-8 technique, which involves inhaling for 4 seconds, holding the breath for 7 seconds, and exhaling slowly for 8 seconds. This method is particularly useful in reducing anxiety and helping with sleep.

Another technique is the box breathing method, favored by athletes and high-performers for its simplicity and effectiveness in stressful situations. Imagine breathing along the sides of a square: Inhale for 4 seconds, hold for 4 seconds, exhale for 4 seconds, and then hold again for 4 seconds. It's a powerful tool for resetting your mental state and preparing for the challenges ahead.

Monday mornings can be particularly tough if you're feeling unprepared or anxious about the upcoming workweek. Utilizing morning breathing exercises can help set a positive tone for the day. A few minutes of mindful breathing can center your thoughts and allow you to tackle your tasks with a calm, focused mindset.

For those who have a hard time winding down Sunday night, try incorporating relaxation breathing techniques before bed. This involves focusing on slow, deep breaths, allowing the belly to rise more than the chest. It aids in calming the nervous system, promoting a restful sleep, and preparing you mentally to face Monday with renewed energy.

It's worth noting the impact of breathing exercises on work performance. When feeling overwhelmed or stressed at work, a few moments dedicated to controlled breathing can vastly improve focus, creativity, and productivity. It serves as a mental reset, clearing the fog of stress, and allowing for clarity and purposeful action.

Breathing exercises can also enhance your work-life balance by establishing boundaries between work stress and personal peace. By practicing breathing techniques, you're consciously creating a buffer that helps keep work-related stress from seeping into your personal life, making your off-work hours more tranquil and enjoyable.

Moreover, these exercises don't require special equipment or significant time investment; they are accessible anytime, anywhere. Whether you're sitting at your desk, in a meeting, or commuting, you can practice these techniques without drawing attention to yourself. It's about carving out moments of mindfulness amidst the chaos of daily work life.

Consistency is key when incorporating breathing exercises into your routine. Make it a habit by setting aside specific times for practice, such as during morning routines, lunch breaks, or right before meetings. Over time, you'll likely notice a decrease in stress levels and an improvement in overall well-being, making Mondays and the rest of the week more manageable.

Incorporating breathing exercises into team settings can also foster a more supportive and positive work environment. Initiating group sessions before starting the workday or important meetings can help reduce collective stress and increase team cohesion. It demonstrates a commitment to not only individual well-being but also to the health of the team dynamic.

Exploring various types of breathing exercises can help you find the methods that work best for you. From guided practices available through apps and online platforms to personalized routines developed with the help of wellness professionals, there's a plethora of resources at your disposal. Experimenting with different techniques allows you to tailor your approach to stress management, ensuring it fits seamlessly into your lifestyle.

Remember, the goal of these exercises is not to eliminate stress entirely but to manage it effectively. Life, with its inevitable ups and downs, will always present challenges. However, by mastering the art of controlled breathing, you equip yourself with a powerful ally in navigating these challenges with grace and resilience.

Breathing exercises offer a simple, yet remarkably effective, way to combat the Monday blues. By incorporating these practices into your daily routine, you can improve your emotional and physical well-being, enhance work performance, and foster a positive work-life balance. Start small, be consistent, and watch as the transformative power of breath changes your approach to Mondays.

Embrace the journey of mastering your breath, and let it lead you to a place of calm, focus, and renewed strength, ready to take on the week ahead with confidence and poise. Monday blues don't stand a chance against the power of mindful breathing.

Muscle Relaxation Techniques

Embarking on a journey to eradicate the Monday blues, it's crucial to discuss the potency of muscle relaxation techniques. When stress oozes into our Sunday evenings, prepping for the week can feel like gearing up for battle rather than welcoming new opportunities. It's in these moments, harnessing control over our physical tension becomes not just beneficial but essential.

Progressive Muscle Relaxation (PMR) stands as a beacon of relief amid the tumultuous waves of anxiety and stress often accompanying the onset of the workweek. This technique entails a two-step process where you tense each muscle group vigorously but without straining, then suddenly release the tension and feel the muscle relax deeply.

The beauty of PMR lies in its simplicity and the immediate sense of relaxation it brings. Beginning with the muscles in your toes and working your way up to your neck and head, you can methodically unwind your entire body, segment by segment. What's remarkable is how this deliberate tension and release can make us acutely aware of where we hold stress and teach our bodies how to let go of it.

Another technique, often overlooked yet incredibly effective, is Deep Touch Pressure (DTP). This involves applying gentle, hands-on pressure to your body to relax the nervous system. Think of the comforting embrace of a hug or the soothing pressure from a weighted blanket. These actions signal safety to our brain, prompting a cascade of relaxation throughout the body and fostering a sense of wellbeing.

Yoga, with its rich history and variety, offers more than just flexibility and strength; it's a treasure trove of relaxation techniques tailor-made for unwinding the knots of stress. The gentle stretching combined with mindful breathing can work wonders, easing muscular tension and clearing the mind. It's a holistic approach to preparing both mind and body for the challenges ahead.

Tai Chi, often described as meditation in motion, is another gem. This ancient martial art focuses on slow, deliberate movements and deep breathing. Embracing Tai Chi on a Monday morning can shift your perspective on the day, moving you from a place of tension and dread to one of calmness and focus. It's about finding balance in motion, a vital skill for tackling weekly tasks.

Visualization techniques complement physical relaxation methods beautifully. Imagine each muscle group relaxing with every exhale. Picture tension melting away like ice under the sun. This mental imagery can significantly amplify the effects of muscle relaxation techniques, paving the way for a serene start to your day.

Autogenic training, though less known, is a powerful self-relaxation technique. It involves repeating a set of visualizations and phrases in your mind to induce a state of relaxation. By focusing on warmth and heaviness in different parts of the body, this method can effectively reduce muscle tension and mental stress.

Implementing these muscle relaxation techniques requires consistency but minimal time investment. Just a few minutes of PMR or DTP before starting your day, or a short session of yoga or Tai Chi, can significantly impact your stress levels and overall outlook. The key is to make it a regular part of your routine, transforming it from a task to a beneficial habit.

To truly reap the benefits, it's important to create a calming environment whenever you engage in these practices. This could mean dimming the lights, playing soft music, or ensuring you're in a comfortable space. Such an atmosphere enhances the relaxation process, making it more effective and enjoyable.

While the physical aspects of these techniques are remarkable, their psychological benefits cannot be overstated. Reducing physical tension has a direct correlation with decreasing mental stress, anxiety, and improving mood. It's a dual-action approach that tackles Monday blues from both fronts.

Integrating muscle relaxation into your lifestyle could be transformative. It's not just about combating Monday blues but adopting a practice that enriches your quality of life, enhances your productivity, and infuses your weekdays with a sense of peace and focus that perhaps was previously amiss.

Muscle relaxation techniques are not a one-off fix but a pathway to a more balanced, focused, and fulfilling work life. They're a testament to the power of taking proactive steps towards not just surviving but thriving in our personal and professional lives. As we tread through each week, these practices can be the anchor that keeps us grounded, reminding us of our resilience and capability to navigate through stress with grace and ease.

Remember, the goal is not to add another cumbersome task to your already packed schedule but to provide a tool that brings relief and rejuvenation. It's about giving yourself permission to pause, even if momentarily, and focus on your wellbeing. So, on the eve of a new week, let's embrace these techniques not as mere exercises but as rituals that nurture our mind, body, and spirit, setting the stage for a week filled with promise, productivity, and peace.

Listening to Music or Podcasts

When it comes to combating the Monday blues, many overlook the simple yet profound impact that listening to music or podcasts can have on our overall mood and outlook, especially as we start a new week. Imagine filling your morning with melodies or conversations that not only entertain but also inspire and motivate you. This isn't just about blocking out the world; it's about intentionally choosing a soundtrack that elevates your spirit and mindset.

Music has an almost magical ability to affect our emotions. The right playlist can energize us, help us focus, or even soothe our anxiety, making it a powerful ally in our quest to beat the Monday blues. Think about how a particular song can transport you, evoke memories, or even change your mood instantaneously. This is because music stimulates the release of dopamine, a neurotransmitter associated with pleasure and motivation. So, why not harness this power as you step into your week?

On the other hand, podcasts offer a different kind of solace and stimulation. They can make us feel connected to others, introduce us to new ideas, or simply provide a distraction from the monotony or stress of a Monday morning. Whether you're into history, comedy, self-improvement, or mysterious stories, there's a podcast out there for you. By immersing yourself in a podcast, you engage your mind in a way that can make your commute or morning routine more enjoyable and stimulating.

Integrating music or podcasts into your Monday routine requires intentionality. The night before, consider what you might need to hear the following morning. Is it motivation, calmness, or perhaps a dose of positivity? Choose your playlist or podcast episode accordingly. This small act of self-care sets a positive tone for the rest of the day and helps you establish control over your mood and outlook.

For those with a longer commute, podcasts can be particularly beneficial. They're an excellent way to make use of time that might otherwise feel wasted or frustrating. Engaging with a podcast can also lessen the feeling of isolation that can accompany the start of the week, providing a sense of connection to the larger world.

Creating specific playlists for your moods or tasks can also be a game-changer. Maybe you have a 'Monday Motivation' playlist filled with energetic songs to kickstart your day or a 'Calming Tunes' playlist for when you need to ease anxiety and find focus. Tailoring your music library in this way makes it easier to find just what you need, when you need it, without spending precious morning minutes scrolling through songs.

For those looking to truly elevate their Monday mornings, consider exploring binaural beats or soundscapes designed to enhance focus, creativity, or relaxation. This type of audio can create an environment conducive to productivity and calm, both crucial for tackling Monday blues.

Let's not overlook the potential for learning and personal growth that podcasts offer. There are countless episodes out there dedicated to self-improvement, motivation, and tackling challenges. Starting your Monday with actionable advice or inspirational stories can empower you to tackle the week ahead with a renewed sense of purpose.

Incorporating music or podcasts into your morning routine doesn't have to be a solitary activity. Sharing a playlist with family or colleagues can create a sense of community and shared experience. Discussing a podcast episode can spark interesting conversations and deepen connections, making the start of the week something to look forward to rather than dread.

Practicality is key in making this habit stick. Ensure your chosen platform is easily accessible and set up your selection the night before. Simplifying the process means you're more likely to stick with it and reap the benefits.

Avoid falling into the trap of listening to content that is likely to exacerbate any stress or anxiety you might be feeling. Curate your playlists and podcast subscriptions with care, opting for content that uplifts and supports your mental and emotional well-being.

Remember, the goal is to use music and podcasts as tools to transform your Mondays from a day of dread to a day filled with potential and positivity. It's about creating moments of joy, inspiration, and comfort as you navigate the day's challenges.

Finally, stay open to experimenting with different genres of music or types of podcasts. Sometimes, stepping out of your auditory comfort zone can lead to discoveries that resonate with you in ways you might not have expected. This openness to new experiences is itself a powerful antidote to the monotony and disheartenment often associated with Mondays.

The strategic use of music and podcasts is more than a mere distraction from the Monday blues; it's an active engagement of your senses, guiding your emotional and mental state towards a place of empowerment and readiness. By making deliberate choices about what you listen to, you're not just passing time, you're crafting an environment that supports your well-being and success.

Journaling

Imagine setting the tone for a week where Monday blues no longer hold dominion over your spirit and ambition. Journaling, an often underutilized tool, can serve as a beacon of self-awareness and transformation, guiding you through the murky waters of Monday discontent with grace and ease. By embracing the pen and paper, or perhaps a digital equivalent, you're not only documenting thoughts but also architecting a resilient mindset that embraces challenges as opportunities for growth.

Embarking on a journaling journey starts with identifying the specific triggers of your Monday blues. Is it the abrupt transition from the freedom of the weekend to the structured demands of the workweek? Or perhaps it's rooted in a lack of motivation or deep-seated dissatisfaction with your job. Recording these feelings and observations can illuminate patterns and root causes, offering clarity and a sense of direction.

But how does one transform this awareness into action? Consider starting each entry with a gratitude list. Highlighting moments of joy and accomplishment, no matter how small, can shift your perspective from what's lacking to the abundance present in your life. This positive reinforcement can be particularly empowering on Sunday evenings, setting a hopeful tone for the week ahead.

Setting goals can also demystify the daunting landscape of the week. When you jot down what you wish to achieve, be it completing specific tasks or dedicating time to self-care, these goals serve as a roadmap, making the week appear more manageable and less overwhelming. The act of writing inspires these intentions with a sense of commitment, transforming abstract aspirations into tangible targets.

Reflection plays a pivotal role in this process. At the end of each day, and especially on Mondays, take a moment to reflect on what went well and the lessons learned from the challenges faced. This practice cultivates a growth mindset, encouraging resilience and adaptability—qualities essential for navigating the complexities of the workweek with grace.

A critical aspect of journaling is addressing the episodes of anxiety and depression that may amplify the Monday blues. Through writing, one can dissect these emotions, understanding their origins and triggers. This self-therapy of sorts provides a private space to confront and process feelings that are often brushed aside in the hustle of daily life.

Moving beyond self-reflection, journaling can also be a means to manifest one's desires and aspirations. The practice of scripting your life as you wish it to unfold—the dream job, the work-life harmony, the eradication of the Monday blues—can be incredibly powerful. This form of positive visualization plants the seeds of motivation and purpose, propelling you forward with renewed vigor and enthusiasm.

For those concerned about the feasibility of incorporating journaling into their routine, the approach need not be time-consuming or laborious. Even a few minutes dedicated to writing before bedtime or in the morning can yield significant benefits. The key is consistency and honesty, allowing yourself the freedom to express your thoughts and feelings without self-censorship.

The beauty of journaling lies in its flexibility; there are no rules carved in stone. Some may prefer structured prompts to guide their writing, while others might find stream-of-consciousness writing more liberating. Experimenting with different styles can uncover what resonates best with you, optimizing the therapeutic and motivational potential of journaling.

Incorporating creative elements, such as sketches or photographs, can further enrich the journaling experience. These visual aids serve not only as a vibrant chronicling of your journey but also as a source of inspiration, reminding you of the progress made and the hurdles overcome.

Moreover, journaling fosters a profound connection with oneself, encouraging introspection and self-discovery. This intimate dialogue can unveil hidden strengths and passions, guiding you toward a career path that aligns with your values and aspirations, thus mitigating the dread associated with Mondays.

Technology has also expanded the horizons of journaling. Various apps offer convenient platforms for capturing thoughts and reflections on the go, ensuring that your journal is always within reach. This digital approach can complement traditional methods, offering a seamless way to integrate journaling into your daily life.

Sharing excerpts from your journal with trusted friends or colleagues can open doors to meaningful conversations and mutual support. This collective engagement not only deepens connections but also broadens perspectives, offering new insights into shared struggles and triumphs.

Finally, reviewing past journal entries can be a source of encouragement and insight. Witnessing your personal growth over time, the challenges surmounted, and the gradual fading of the Monday blues into a more vibrant and hopeful outlook is nothing short of invigorating. This retrospective journey underscores the transformative power of journaling, reinforcing its value as a companion in your quest for a fulfilling and balanced life.

Journaling serves as a mighty sword in the battle against the Monday blues. By fostering self-awareness, goal setting, positive reflection, and personal growth, it equips you to face Mondays—and indeed every day—with a sense of purpose, strength, and optimism. Let the pages of your journal be a testament to your journey, a celebration of overcoming, and a roadmap to a future where Mondays are welcomed with open arms and a resilient heart.

Using Affirmations

Transforming the dread of Monday starts with transforming our thoughts. Affirmations, simple yet powerful statements, can be the key to shifting our mindset and conquering the Monday blues. They serve as reminders of our capabilities, strengths, and goals, steering our focus away from the negatives and towards positive, actionable intentions.

It's natural to be skeptical about the power of repeating positive statements. However, the practice goes beyond mere repetition; affirmations help reprogram our subconscious mind, gradually replacing our pattern of negative thoughts with a more optimistic outlook. This doesn't happen overnight but integrating affirmations into our daily routine can lead to remarkable shifts in our attitude and perceptions over time.

To begin, select affirmations that resonate with your personal and professional goals. These could range from statements that address self-esteem, such as "I am competent, smart, and able," to affirmations that focus on productivity and enthusiasm, like "I am fully engaged and excited about today's challenges."

Consistency is key. Affirmations are most effective when practiced daily. Incorporating them into your morning routine can set a positive tone for the day ahead. Try repeating them while you prepare for work or during your commute. The goal is to make these positive affirmations the first thoughts that guide your mindset at the start of each week.

Visualization enhances the effectiveness of affirmations. While reciting your affirmations, picture yourself achieving the outcomes you're affirming. Imagine conquering your tasks, feeling energized, and receiving praise for your hard work. This process not only boosts your mood but also prepares you mentally to tackle the day's challenges.

Writing down your affirmations can reinforce their impact. Keeping a journal where you record and revisit your affirmations helps solidify these positive statements in your mind. Occasionally, reflect on the affirmations you've written and note any progress or shifts in your mindset. This reflective practice can be incredibly rewarding and motivating.

Sharing affirmations with a friend or colleague can also be beneficial. This creates a support system where you encourage and uplift each other, making it easier to face Mondays with a positive outlook. Plus, hearing affirmations from someone else can often make them more impactful.

Don't be discouraged if you don't notice immediate changes. The effect of affirmations is cumulative. Over time, you'll find that your automatic thoughts begin to lean more towards positivity and resilience, making it easier to bounce back from setbacks and approach Mondays with vigor.

Customize affirmations to address specific aspects of the Monday blues. If you struggle with feeling overwhelmed by the workload, affirmations like "I handle my responsibilities with ease and calm" can be particularly soothing. If it's a lack of motivation you battle with, something along the lines of "I am filled with energy and enthusiasm for my work" might serve you better.

Technology can aid in reinforcing affirmations. There are several apps available that remind you to practice your affirmations. Additionally, setting up reminders or alarms on your phone with a daily affirmation can integrate this practice seamlessly into your life.

It's also important to align your actions with your affirmations. While affirming your productivity and enthusiasm, ensure that you're setting up your day to reflect these qualities. This might mean organizing your workspace, prioritizing tasks, or simply taking a moment to breathe and center yourself before diving into your day.

Affirmations should be in the present tense, focusing on what you are achieving and becoming. Sentences that start with "I am" are powerful and serve as strong declarations of your current state and aspirations. This helps reinforce the belief that you are capable of overcoming the challenges of Mondays—and every other day, for that matter.

It's also beneficial to remain open to adjusting your affirmations as your goals and needs evolve. Your journey towards a more fulfilling work life is dynamic, so your affirmations should reflect your current aspirations and challenges. Revisiting and revising your affirmations keeps them relevant and impactful.

Using affirmations as a tool to combat Monday blues is about cultivating a mindset of positivity and resilience. While it may require patience and persistence, the gradual shift in outlook can significantly affect both your professional and personal life. Embarking on this journey of positive self-talk not only helps eliminate the Monday blues but also aids in achieving a greater sense of fulfillment and balance in every aspect of life.

Taking Breaks

Imagine starting your Monday equipped with a strategy so powerful, it transforms the dread of the beginning of the week into an energized leap out of bed. At the heart of this strategy lies the simple, yet often overlooked practice of taking breaks. Crafting a break schedule that suits your Monday mood can not only elevate your spirits but significantly enhance your productivity and focus.

Understanding the essence of what breaks do can illuminate why they're so crucial. Breaks serve as mental palate cleansers, offering your brain a momentary respite from the cognitive loads it carries. A well-timed break recharges the brain, enabling you to return to tasks with renewed focus and vitality. This is particularly helpful on Mondays when your mind might still be meandering through the remnants of the weekend.

But not all breaks are created equal. The secret to a rejuvenating break lies in its quality. A high-quality break is one that truly allows your mind to wander away from work-related thoughts. It might involve a short walk, a mindfulness exercise, or simply sitting quietly while savoring a cup of coffee. The activity matters less than the mental detachment it provides.

Timing is also critical. Research suggests that the human brain works optimally by following cycles of concentrated work followed by short periods of rest. Pomodoro, a popular time management technique, advocates for 25 minutes of focused work followed by a 5-minute break. However, the exact timing can be flexible; the key is to listen to your body's cues. Feeling fatigued, distracted, or frustrated are all signs that it's time for a break.

Integrating break times into your Monday routine can start with small, intentional steps. Begin by scheduling at least three short breaks throughout your day, dedicating them to activities that help you disconnect momentarily. As you grow more accustomed to these pauses, experiment with their length and frequencies to find what best energizes you.

Moreover, consider the environment of your breaks. Stepping away from your usual workspace, if possible, can enhance the effectiveness of your downtime. A change of scenery, even as simple as moving to a different room, can provide a refreshing change in perspective, helping you to mentally reset.

It's also valuable to engage in physical movement during breaks. Stretching, a quick walk around the block, or even some light yoga can help release muscle tension built up from hours of sitting. This physical activity not only boosts your energy levels but can also enhance mental clarity and combat afternoon fatigue, which is often at its peak on Mondays.

Adopting a mindful approach to breaks can transform them into moments of gratitude and reflection. Instead of scrolling through your phone, consider jotting down a few things you're grateful for or engaging in a brief meditation session. These practices can foster a positive mindset, equipping you with resilience to face Monday's challenges.

Don't forget to hydrate and nourish your body during breaks. Snacking on healthy foods and staying hydrated can have a surprisingly positive effect on your mood and energy levels. The slump many experience on Monday afternoons can often be mitigated by proper nutrition and hydration.

For those who may find it challenging to remember to take breaks, technology can come to the rescue. Numerous apps are designed to gently remind you to pause and breathe. Alternatively, setting reminders on your phone or computer can serve the same purpose, helping embed break-taking into your Monday routine.

Respecting your breaks is essential. It's tempting to cut breaks short or skip them altogether, especially when faced with mounting Monday tasks. However, remember that breaks are not a luxury; they're a necessity for sustained productivity. Honor your scheduled breaks just as you would a meeting with a colleague.

Sharing the concept of taking breaks with teammates or family members can foster a supportive environment that encourages everyone to prioritize their well-being. This collective acknowledgment of the importance of breaks can create a more harmonious and productive work and home life, especially at the start of the week.

Lastly, be patient and kind to yourself as you integrate more intentional breaks into your Mondays. It might take some time to discover the types of breaks that most effectively uplift and rejuvenate you. This exploration is part of the journey toward mastering your Mondays, transforming them from a day of dread to one of opportunity and growth.

In conclusion, the art of taking breaks is a powerful tool in battling the Monday blues. Thoughtfully integrating breaks into your day can not only transform your Mondays but also significantly improve your overall work-life balance and job performance. By honoring your need for rest and rejuvenation, you equip yourself to tackle each week with renewed energy and a fresh perspective.

Emphasizing Work/Life Balance

Stepping into a space where work and personal life harmoniously blend can seem like a monumentally daunting task, especially when the dreadful Monday blues hit hard. But have you ever thought about the transformative impact of prioritizing a work/life balance? It's about creating a fulfilling and manageable routine that allows you to thrive both inside and outside of your professional endeavors. Let's dive deeper into why and how cultivating this balance is crucial for eliminating Monday blues.

First and foremost, it's essential to recognize that work doesn't define our entire existence. While it's a significant part of our lives, allowing it to overshadow other aspects can lead to feelings of burnout and dissatisfaction, which are often most acute at the start of the week. By consciously dedicating time to our hobbies, families, and wellbeing, we create a buffer against the stress and routine of work.

A pivotal strategy in achieving work/life balance involves setting clear boundaries between work and personal time. This could mean turning off work-related notifications and choosing not to check emails during evenings or weekends. It's about giving yourself permission to unplug and recharge, ensuring that work doesn't encroach on your personal space.

Moreover, effective time management plays a crucial role. It's not just about managing your work tasks efficiently but also about making deliberate choices on how to spend your personal time. Structuring your day to include activities that bring joy and relaxation can significantly impact your overall mood and reduce the dread of Monday mornings.

Incorporating flexibility into your work schedule can also be a game-changer. If your job allows, exploring options like remote work or flexible hours can help manage personal obligations more smoothly, reducing stress and enhancing productivity both at work and home.

Another vital component is mindfulness. Taking moments throughout the day to practice mindfulness or meditation can help in staying grounded and centered, despite the pressures that come with balancing work and personal life. It's about being present in the moment and dealing with stress in a healthy, constructive way.

Physical activity is another cornerstone of maintaining a healthy work/life balance. Exercise not only improves your physical health but also boosts mental clarity, mood, and resilience against stress. Carving out time for regular physical activity can be especially beneficial in recalibrating your mood and energy levels for the week ahead.

Social connections are equally significant. Make it a point to spend quality time with loved ones and nurture relationships outside of your work circle. Strong social ties contribute to a sense of belonging and support, powering you through challenging days, including those Monday blues.

Don't forget the power of pursuing passions and hobbies outside of work. Engaging in activities that you're passionate about recharges your batteries and offers a refreshing break from work-related concerns, making you more energized and motivated when Monday rolls around.

Sleep, undoubtedly, is an imperative factor in achieving work/life balance. Ensuring you have a consistent sleep routine can drastically improve your mood, cognitive function, and overall health. Prioritizing sleep is prioritizing your ability to perform at your best both at work and in your personal life.

Learning to say "no" is also a critical aspect of fostering work/life balance. It's vital to set realistic expectations for what you can achieve and communicate these boundaries effectively. Taking on too much can easily lead to stress and burnout, exacerbating Monday blues.

Reflecting on and adjusting your priorities on a regular basis is key. What's important today might not be so tomorrow. As your personal and professional goals evolve, so too should your approach to balancing these aspects of your life.

Remember, achieving a satisfying work/life balance is a continuous process, not a one-time fix. It requires constant adjustment and mindfulness but can significantly mitigate the Monday blues. By valuing your personal time as much as your professional time, you cultivate a life where Mondays are no longer a source of stress but an opportunity for fresh beginnings and renewed focus.

It's time to redefine what Mondays mean to us. By emphasizing work/life balance, we're not just improving our disdain for Mondays; we're enhancing our overall quality of life. So let's embrace the necessary changes and steps to create a harmonious balance that serves us all week long, including those daunting Mondays.

Combating Monday blues starts with a comprehensive approach to work/life balance. It's about making intentional choices every day that align with our well-being, happiness, and productivity. When we start seeing our work and personal life not as competitors but as complementary parts of our whole self, we unlock the potential to experience Mondays, and indeed every day, with a positive and balanced outlook.

Scheduling Something Fun

The familiar dread of Monday can cast a shadow over even the most enjoyable Sundays. Yet, it's within our power to change that narrative and inject a hint of anticipation into our Mondays. One simple, yet profoundly transformative approach is to schedule something fun at the start of your week. This isn't just about distraction; it's about reprogramming our perception of Mondays from a day of stress to a beacon of joy.

Imagine beginning your week not with a groan, but with a sense of excitement. It's about crafting moments that fuel your spirit and set a positive tone for the days to come. Whether it's a small treat or an activity you genuinely love, the psychological lift it provides can significantly alter how you view and experience the rest of your week.

Consider for a moment the power of anticipation. Just the act of looking forward to a pleasant event can elevate your mood and improve your overall outlook. By scheduling something enjoyable on a Monday, you're not only giving yourself a delightful experience but also leveraging the psychological benefits of anticipation to make your entire week seem more promising.

What constitutes "fun" can vary wildly from person to person. For some, it might mean booking a class in something you've always wanted to learn. It could be art, dance, or perhaps a new language. The key is to choose an activity that resonates with you, something that sparks joy and ignites your passion.

Others might find their fun in quieter, more introspective activities. Meditation groups, a solo hike, or even dedicating time to read a chapter of a book in a favorite café can transform your Monday from mundane to something you genuinely look forward to.

Let's not forget the communal aspect of fun. Sometimes, the best way to start the week is by connecting with others. This could be a weekly breakfast date with a friend, a movie night, or starting a book club. The idea is to create a sense of community and shared experiences that enrich your life and those around you.

But it's important to note that scheduling something fun isn't a one-size-fits-all solution. It requires intentionality and a bit of creativity. It's about identifying what truly brings you joy and finding inventive ways to weave those elements into your Monday routine.

Practicality is also key. While it's tempting to plan elaborate events, simplicity often yields the greatest joy. It can be as uncomplicated as cooking a special meal or watching a sunrise.

The complexity of the activity matters less than the happiness it brings.

Moreover, this strategy goes beyond mere enjoyment. It's a powerful tool for enhancing work-life balance. By anchoring your week with activities that you're passionate about, it blurs the rigid lines between personal and professional life, creating a more harmonious blend.

Resistance to this idea might arise, fueled by the belief that there's simply no time for fun at the start of a busy week. However, this is where the realignment of priorities comes into play. It's about recognizing that your well-being is paramount and understanding that making time for joy can significantly impact your productivity and job performance.

In essence, scheduling something fun on Monday is an act of self-care—an acknowledgment that your needs matter and a proactive step towards meeting them. It's a reminder that life is meant to be enjoyed, not just endured, and that even the most dreaded days can be transformed into opportunities for growth and happiness.

As you embark on this journey, remember to be flexible. Not every fun activity will be a perfect fit, and that's okay. The goal is to explore and discover what energizes you, what helps you start your week with a spark of joy, and what keeps the Monday blues at bay.

Bear in mind that this practice, like any other, takes consistency to yield results. Initially, the change might feel awkward or forced, but over time, you'll likely discover that Mondays can be just as enjoyable as Fridays. The dread once associated with the start of the week can be replaced with enthusiasm, transforming not just your Mondays, but your perception of what every week can bring.

By scheduling something fun at the start of your week, you're not only combating the Monday blues but also enriching your life with moments of joy and fulfillment. It's a testament to the power of positive anticipation and a practical step towards creating a more balanced, enjoyable life. So, go ahead, plan something delightful for your next Monday. Your future self will thank you for it.

Working Remotely or Using Flexible Schedules

As we pivot from understanding the depths of Monday blues to actionable strategies for alleviating them, a significant aspect worth considering is the dynamic nature of work schedules. The traditional 9-to-5, Monday-to-Friday workweek, while still prevalent, may not be the ideal fit for everyone. In this ever-evolving professional landscape, the option to work remotely or adopt flexible schedules stands out as a beacon of hope for many aiming to enhance their work-life balance and, subsequently, eradicate Monday blues.

Remote work and flexible hours offer a breath of fresh air for those stifled by the rigidity of conventional office settings. Imagine a morning where you're not battling traffic but instead, beginning your day with a quiet coffee at your preferred pace. This relaxed start can have profound effects on your mental health and overall attitude towards Mondays.

Furthermore, the autonomy that comes with dictating your work hours or environment can significantly boost your productivity. It's about working when you feel most creative and energetic, rather than being confined to a schedule that might not align with your personal peak performance times. This way, the dread of Monday mornings can be mitigated, as you have the power to shape your day in a way that suits you best.

Adopting a flexible schedule also allows for better personal time management. No longer are personal appointments or family commitments a source of stress, as you can design your work schedule around these important aspects of life. This flexibility can decrease the likelihood of feeling overwhelmed or burnt out, common contributors to the Monday blues.

Yet, it's essential to acknowledge that working remotely or on flexible schedules requires a high level of self-discipline and organization. The boundaries between work and personal life can blur, potentially leading to longer work hours if not carefully managed. Establishing a dedicated workspace, setting clear work hours, and adhering to a routine are critical for maintaining productivity and ensuring that the newfound flexibility serves its intended purpose of improving your quality of life.

Effective communication with your employer and colleagues is equally important in making flexible work arrangements successful. Clear expectations regarding availability, meeting times, and project deadlines help ensure that everyone is on the same page, thus minimizing misunderstandings and maintaining professional relationships.

One might wonder if this flexibility affects team cohesion or company culture. On the contrary, when implemented thoughtfully, it can lead to a more satisfied and engaged workforce. Employees who feel their personal time is respected tend to exhibit higher levels of loyalty and motivation, which can, in turn, enhance teamwork and productivity.

Employers also stand to gain from offering remote work or flexible schedules. Access to a broader talent pool, reduced office space requirements, and potentially lower turnover rates are just a few of the benefits. Moreover, companies that embrace these practices are often viewed as more progressive and employee-friendly, which can significantly boost their employer brand.

It's worth noting that remote work and flexible hours are not one-size-fits-all solutions. Some people may thrive in a structured office environment, finding it easier to focus and collaborate. However, for those who suffer from severe Monday blues, the flexibility to tailor their work environment and schedule can be a game-changer.

To successfully implement a flexible working arrangement, it's crucial to start with a trial period. This allows both the employee and employer to assess the effectiveness of the arrangement and make adjustments as needed. It's also an excellent opportunity to develop personal strategies for staying productive and balancing work with life's other responsibilities.

Technology plays a pivotal role in making remote work and flexible schedules feasible. Utilizing project management tools, video conferencing, and cloud-based applications can help maintain productivity and foster collaboration, irrespective of physical location.

The transition to remote work or flexible schedules can be a potent antidote to the Monday blues. It offers a more personalized work approach, acknowledging and adapting to individual preferences and life commitments. However, it requires a strong foundation of self-discipline, organizational skills, and effective communication. For those feeling trapped by the Monday blues, exploring these options could very well be the key to unlocking a happier, more balanced professional life.

As we navigate the complexities of modern work environments, it's clear that flexibility and autonomy over one's schedule can significantly contribute to a more positive outlook on Mondays. By redefining what the start of the workweek looks like, we can transform it from a source of dread to an opportunity for growth, productivity, and satisfaction.

In the following chapters, we will delve deeper into more strategies to combat Monday blues and enhance job satisfaction. By considering flexible work arrangements as part of a broader approach to improving work-life balance, we open the door to a future where Monday blues become a thing of the past.

Maintaining Self-Care Habits

Moving forward in our journey to conquer the Monday Blues, an essential stride lies in the nurturing of self-care habits. In a world that demands our constant attention, the art of self-preservation becomes paramount. This chapter delves into the vitality of maintaining self-care routines as a cornerstone for not just improving Mondays, but enhancing life's overall quality.

Self-care is an expansive concept, encompassing a multitude of actions geared towards one's own health and well-being. It's a personalized script that varies distinctly from person to person. For some, self-care could mean carving out time for exercise, indulging in a hobby, or simply ensuring a full night's sleep. The essence, however, remains rooted in doing activities that replenish rather than deplete you.

Initiating a self-care routine demands introspection. It's about identifying what nourishes your soul and what drains it. Begin by carving out moments in your schedule dedicated solely to activities that bring you joy and relaxation. It might seem like a luxury in the rush of weekdays, but it's these moments that build resilience against stress and uplift your spirit.

One cannot stress enough the significance of physical wellness in the grand scheme of self-care. Regular exercise has been shown to improve mood, enhance energy levels, and mitigate symptoms of anxiety and depression. Instituting a routine, be it yoga, running, or simply walking, can serve as a powerful antidote to the dread that often precedes Mondays.

Nutrition plays a crucial role in how we feel, both physically and emotionally. A diet that prioritizes whole foods over processed options can dramatically affect our energy levels and mood. Preparing nutritious meals for the week ahead is not just a step towards physical health but a form of self-respect and an investment in your future self.

Ensuring adequate sleep is another pillar of self-care often compromised. The quality of our sleep directly influences our cognitive function, mood, and overall health. Establishing a calming pre-sleep routine can significantly improve the quality of rest, thereby equipping us with a refreshed and renewed mindset to tackle the week ahead.

Mental and emotional self-care are as vital as the physical aspect. Practices such as meditation, journaling, and gratitude exercises can help in maintaining a healthy mental state. Allocating time for these activities, especially on Sundays or Mondays, can set a positive tone for the week and aid in navigating through it with a grounded and resilient outlook.

The company we keep influences our energy and outlook tremendously. Surrounding ourselves with supportive and positive individuals can act as a buffer against the Monday blues. Cultivating relationships that encourage and uplift you is an integral part of self-care that extends its benefits well beyond individual wellbeing.

In an era where digital connectivity is omnipresent, digital detoxes have become an essential self-care practice. Setting aside time to unplug from electronic devices and social media can help in reducing anxiety, improving attention span, and enhancing one's connection with the immediate physical environment.

Another overlooked aspect of self-care is the setting of boundaries – both personal and professional. It's crucial to recognize your limits and communicate them effectively. Learning to say 'no' when necessary can prevent overcommitment, burnout, and preserve one's energy for activities that are truly fulfilling.

Engaging in creative pursuits can be a profoundly therapeutic component of self-care. Whether it's painting, writing, gardening, or playing music, creative expression allows for a unique form of escapism and provides a channel for processing emotions and stress in a constructive manner.

Self-compassion and kindness towards oneself are foundational to self-care. It's important to treat yourself with the same empathy and understanding that you would offer a friend. Acknowledging your efforts, forgiving your missteps, and celebrating your progress, no matter how small, can foster a sense of inner peace and satisfaction.

While establishing and maintaining self-care habits requires effort and commitment, the return on this investment is substantial. By prioritizing your own well-being, you not only enhance your capacity to tackle Mondays with vigor but also elevate your overall quality of life. It's about making a conscious choice daily to engage in practices that nourish rather than negate your well-being.

Self-care is not a one-time task but a continuous journey. It's about making small, sustainable changes that cumulatively enrich your life. As we navigate through the nuances of overcoming Monday blues, remember that at the heart of this endeavor lies the simple, yet profound act of taking care of oneself. So, let's embrace self-care not as an act of indulgence but as a critical component of our overall strategy to live a more balanced, content, and fulfilling life.

As we close this chapter, reflect on the self-care practices you currently engage in and consider new ones that might bring additional joy and resilience into your life. The path to mitigating Monday blues and enhancing your work-life experience significantly involves honoring and taking care of the most important person in this equation – you.

Remembering Your Purpose

As we navigate the complexities of eliminating Monday blues, an essential element demands our attention: remembering your purpose. It's the compass that guides us through the most turbulent storms and the beacon that lights our darkest nights. In the hustle of our Mondays, it becomes all too easy to lose sight of why we do what we do. But, it's in the remembrance of our purpose that we find the strength to conquer any gloom that Mondays might bring.

Think of your purpose as the engine of your motivation. When Monday morning rolls around, and the bed feels too warm, and the world too cold, it's your purpose that whispers, "There's more to this." It nudges you forward, reminding you that each task, no matter how mundane, connects to a larger goal, a dream, or aspiration that set your heart on fire once. It's crucial, then, to keep this purpose not just alive but vibrant within us.

But how does one remember their purpose, especially when ensnared by the fog of Monday blues? First, it's about establishing a clear vision. Sit down and articulate what drives you. Is it to provide for your family? To make a dent in your corner of the universe? To create something that lasts? Write it down. Make it tangible. Something you can hold onto when the going gets tough.

Visualization plays a pivotal role here. Imagine achieving your goals. Let the image of you, living your purpose, fill your mind. This visualization acts as a lighthouse, guiding you back to your path whenever you stray. Every morning, and especially on Mondays, spend a few moments basking in this visualization. Feel the emotions, savor the triumphs, solidify your purpose in your heart and mind.

Another crucial aspect is setting purpose-driven goals for each Monday. Break down your larger purpose into actionable steps. Perhaps your overarching purpose is to influence positive change in your industry. What step can you take this Monday to move closer to that goal? This approach ensures that even the smallest tasks are imbued with meaning, transforming mundane to-dos into purposeful actions.

Moreover, it's often the case that we forget to reflect on our journey. Continuous reflection helps us to not only appreciate how far we've come but also to realign our actions with our true purpose. It can be as simple as keeping a journal where you jot down thoughts and feelings about your work and your purpose at the end of each day. Over time, you'll see patterns, progress, and possibly areas where you've veered off path, providing the insight needed to correct course.

Seeking connection with others who share your purpose or can relate to your journey is another potent method to keep the flame of your purpose alive. Whether it's a mentor, peer, or online community, expressing your goals, challenges, and triumphs can bolster your commitment to your purpose. It creates a support system, a network of cheerleaders and advisors who can remind you of your 'why' when you need it the most.

It's also about practicing gratitude. Remembering to be grateful for the opportunities and challenges alike resets your mental state, shifting focus from what's going wrong to what's going right. This practice fosters a positive mindset that's conducive to remembering and pursuing your purpose with vigor.

Additionally, embracing adaptability is key. Our purposes might evolve as we grow, and that's perfectly okay. Sometimes, the feeling of disconnection from our work indicates that our purpose has shifted, and we need to recalibrate. Stay open to this evolution and see it as an opportunity to dive deeper into understanding what truly moves you.

On a practical note, integrate your purpose into your daily life. Make it visible. It could be a motivational quote on your desk, a picture of your loved ones, or a note pinned to your computer monitor - whatever symbolizes your 'why'. This constant visual reminder serves as a tool to swiftly bring you back to your purpose, especially on challenging days.

Leveraging your purpose as a tool against Monday blues requires commitment. It's not a passive process but an active pursuit. Wake up every morning, especially on Mondays, with the intention to live purposefully. Remind yourself of your 'why' before even stepping out of bed. This mindset frames your entire day through the lens of purpose, infusing even the smallest actions with significance.

Moreover, infuse purpose into your breaks and downtime. Even your moments of rest can be aligned with your purpose. Whether it's reading a book related to your goals, meditating on your aspirations, or simply enjoying a hobby that recharges your batteries for the mission ahead. This ensures that your entire day, not just the work hours, contributes to your overall sense of purpose.

In this journey, remember that setbacks are part of the process. There will be Mondays where your purpose feels distant, almost like a mirage. It's in these moments that the true challenge lies. Embrace these setbacks as opportunities for growth. Reflect on them, learn from them, and let them enlarge your capacity to persevere towards your goals with even greater resolve.

Celebrate every victory, no small feat should go unnoticed. Each step forward, no matter how small, is progress. It's a brick in the foundation of your dreams. Celebrating these victories keeps the momentum going, fueling your journey through even the toughest Mondays.

Remembering your purpose transforms the fight against Monday blues from a battle to a journey—a journey worth every step. It's this purpose that makes Mondays not just bearable, but meaningful, and sets the stage for a fulfilling week ahead. Hold onto it, nurture it, and let it guide you through the inevitable ups and downs. In remembering your purpose, you find the ultimate antidote to Monday blues.

Doing Something You Love

In the grand scheme of conquering Monday blues, pursuing passions within our careers holds unparalleled power. We often hear that doing something you love transforms every day into an opportunity rather than a chore. But how exactly does this relate to eliminating the dread of Mondays? The answer lies in the joy and satisfaction derived from engaging in work that resonates with our inner selves, making the start of the workweek something to look forward to rather than something to survive.

Consider the essence of what it means to do something you love. It's not merely about choosing a job that aligns with your hobbies or interests but finding or creating a role that speaks to your values, strengths, and, ultimately, your purpose. This alignment fosters a sense of accomplishment and contentment, diminishing the stark contrast between the freedom of the weekend and the obligations of the weekday.

Imagine waking up on a Monday morning with a spark of enthusiasm, ready to tackle the challenges and opportunities lying ahead in your workday. This feeling is not a distant dream but a tangible reality for those who have integrated their passions into their professions. The anticipation of contributing to something meaningful can significantly alter our perception of Mondays.

Engaging in work you love also promotes a state of flow, where time seems to fly by as you immerse yourself in tasks that challenge and fulfill you. This psychological state not only boosts productivity but also enhances your well-being, making the usual Monday blues a thing of the past.

Nevertheless, it's important to acknowledge that finding your passion or transitioning to a job that reflects it might not happen overnight. It often requires introspection, experimentation, and a willingness to step outside your comfort zone. Yet, the journey towards doing what you love is in itself enriching, filled with learning and growth that pave the way for a more enjoyable work life.

Moreover, doing something you love doesn't mean you'll never face stress or obstacles on Mondays or any other day. However, the key difference is how you perceive and handle these challenges. When your work aligns with your passions, overcoming hurdles feels more like a rewarding part of the process rather than an insurmountable setback.

Additionally, integrating your interests into your career might involve creative thinking and flexibility. It could mean proposing new projects within your current role that align with your passions or exploring side projects that fulfill you and enhance your main job. This proactive approach not only combats Monday blues but also contributes to your professional development.

The ripple effects of doing what you love extend beyond personal satisfaction. It positively influences your colleagues and workplace culture, inspiring others to pursue their passions and fostering an environment where Mondays are welcomed with optimism and energy.

Furthermore, dedicating yourself to work that you're passionate about often leads to excellence. When we care deeply about what we do, we're more inclined to go the extra mile, innovate, and drive remarkable results. This excellence not only furthers our careers but also injects a sense of pride and joy into our Mondays.

It's also crucial to recognize that passions can evolve. What you love doing today might change in the future, and that's perfectly okay. Embracing this evolution allows you to adapt and find new avenues of joy and fulfillment in your work, keeping the Monday blues at bay no matter where you are in your career journey.

On a practical note, start small by identifying aspects of your job that you enjoy or find meaningful. Focus on incorporating more of these elements into your daily or weekly routine. Every step towards doing something you love is a step away from the dread of Mondays.

To support this transition, seek mentors or communities that align with your interests. They can provide valuable insights, encouragement, and connections to opportunities that resonate with your passions. Remember, no one has to navigate this path alone.

Also, embrace the idea of lifelong learning. Pursuing courses or certifications related to your interests not only enhances your skills but also keeps you engaged and motivated. This commitment to growth can transform every Monday into a fresh start with new possibilities.

Doing something you love is a potent antidote to Monday blues. It's about more than just enjoying your job; it's about connecting with your work on a profound level that enriches your life and ignites your Mondays with purpose and passion. By taking deliberate steps towards this goal, you can redefine the start of your week, turning it into a catalyst for fulfillment and success.

So, let's reframe our approach to Mondays. Instead of bracing for the week ahead, we can embrace it with enthusiasm and resolve, fueled by the work we love. In doing so, we not only enhance our own lives but also contribute to a broader culture of joy, purpose, and inspiration in the workplace. Here's to loving what you do and doing what you love, making every Monday not just bearable, but bright and fulfilling.

Rethinking Your Job

As we navigate the complexities of overcoming the Monday Blues, it's crucial that we take a moment to truly dissect and understand the role our current job plays in our overall satisfaction and happiness. This journey invites us to probe deeper than the surface level frustrations we might encounter on a day-to-day basis. It's about evaluating whether our work aligns with our core values, passions, and the lifestyle we aspire to lead.

At times, the very thought of reconsidering our job's place in our lives can feel daunting, especially if we've invested years into building a career within a particular field. However, it's this attachment to what we've always known that can sometimes blind us to the boundless opportunities waiting just on the horizon. The question isn't merely about whether you like your job; it's about whether your job is adding to your life's narrative in a fulfilling way.

Consider for a moment the aspects of your job that ignite a spark within you. These are often tasks or projects that draw upon your strengths and interests, leaving you feeling accomplished and energized. Now, think about the parts that drain your spirit, the segments of your workday that feel like they're siphoning your zest for life. The balance—or lack thereof—between these two can serve as a powerful indicator of how well your job fits with your intrinsic motivations and long-term goals.

The implications of finding ourselves in roles that don't align with our personal values and aspirations can be profound. It can lead to not just the dreaded Monday Blues, but a continual sense of dissatisfaction that permeates other areas of our lives. This disconnect acts as a barrier to experiencing genuine joy and enthusiasm, not just at the start of the week, but every day.

In rethinking our job, it's not about making impulsive decisions or immediate changes. Rather, it's about starting a dialogue with ourselves about what we truly seek from our professional lives. It's about envisioning a life where work feels less like an obligation and more like an expression of our deepest selves.

To embark on this path of self-discovery, start by listing down what you value most in life. This could range from creativity, making a meaningful impact, to having the flexibility to spend time with loved ones. Once you've pinpointed these values, assess how well your current job aligns with them. This exercise is not about judging your current situation but understanding it more fully.

There's also tremendous power in exploring new opportunities that might better match your identified values and interests. Sometimes, we remain in unsatisfying roles out of fear of the unknown or an overestimation of the risks involved in change. Researching potential career paths, even if purely hypothetical, can help loosen the grip of fear and open your mind to the possibilities.

Networking, both within and outside your current industry, can also offer invaluable insights into other professions. Conversations with others about their journey, challenges, and satisfactions can illuminate paths you hadn't considered or affirm the direction you're contemplating.

Educational opportunities should not be overlooked as well. Whether it's formal education, online courses, or workshops, learning new skills or deepening existing ones can not only boost your resume but also rekindle your love for your profession—or help steer you in a new direction.

Embracing a mindset of growth and exploration can transform the way you think about your job and its role in your life. It's about understanding that it's never too late to align your career with your passions and dreams. The realization that you have the power to effect change in your professional life is both liberating and motivating.

In this process of reevaluation, it's also important to recognize that change doesn't always entail a complete career overhaul. Sometimes, subtle shifts within your current role or company can significantly enhance your job satisfaction. This could mean taking on new projects that align more closely with your interests or negotiating for flexible working conditions that better suit your lifestyle.

Before making any drastic changes, it's wise to consult with trusted mentors, friends, or family members. Their perspectives can provide clarity, offer support, and perhaps even share experiences of their own transitions that might be inspiring or cautionary tales.

The path to finding joy and fulfillment in our professional lives is a deeply personal and ongoing journey. What works for one person may not work for another. The key is to approach this process with an open heart and a curious mind, allowing yourself the space to dream and the courage to pursue those dreams.

Ultimately, rethinking your job is not just about improving your Mondays; it's about reshaping your life to be more vibrant, meaningful, and aligned with who you truly are. It's about creating a work-life symbiosis that energizes and fulfills you, enabling you to live your best life every day of the week.

Remember, the goal here isn't to escape work but to find or create work that doesn't feel like an escape is necessary. Through introspection, exploration, and possibly transformation, you can turn the dread of Monday into anticipation, and in doing so, illuminate the rest of your week—and indeed, your life—with purpose and passion.

Chapter 4:
Pathways to Happiness at Work

As we move beyond the basics of phasing out the Monday Blues, we dive into the essence of what it truly means to find happiness within the confines of our workplaces. Recognizing that happiness at work is not just an elusive goal but a necessary component for a fulfilling life, we start by identifying personal joy. It can be as simple as enjoying your morning coffee in silence before the day begins or as complex as accomplishing challenging tasks that stretch your capabilities. The key is to understand what sparks joy for you personally. This understanding serves as the cornerstone of constructing a more satisfying work life. The importance of introspection cannot be overstated here; it's the beacon that guides you through the fog of daily routines and tasks.

A crucial step in this journey is seeking job satisfaction and fulfillment. This doesn't necessarily mean looking for a new job, although it can. More often, it involves re-evaluating your current role and finding ways to align it more closely with your values, interests, and what you find intrinsically motivating. It's about creating a job that doesn't just pay the bills but enriches your life. Engaging in tasks that challenge you in a positive way, seeking opportunities for growth, and advocating for yourself in the workplace can transform your job from a source of stress to a source of satisfaction. This transformation isn't instantaneous, but with persistent effort and a positive mindset, significant changes are possible.

Rethinking your job and its role in your life is perhaps the most profound step on this journey. It's easy to fall into the trap of defining ourselves by our work. However, seeing your job as just one aspect of your life can free you from undue stress and anxiety. It allows you to find balance and appreciate the role work plays in your life without letting it overshadow everything else. By identifying what you value most in life and seeking to incorporate more of those elements into your daily work, you create a more harmonious existence. The pursuit of happiness at work is fundamentally about finding your place in the world and making peace with it. It's a journey well worth taking.

Identifying What Makes You Happy

As we transition into exploring the multifaceted pathways to achieving happiness at work, a fundamental step is unearthing what truly kindles joy within us. This journey, entirely personal and deeply introspective, requires us to pause and reflect on our current professional life and beyond. Happiness, often perceived as a distant or complex goal, starts with understanding our own needs, desires, and what sparks a sense of fulfillment and satisfaction.

At the core of this exploration is the concept that joy in our professional lives can't be separated from our overall happiness. The two are intrinsically linked, feeding into one another in a cycle that either uplifts or depletes us. Thus, identifying what makes us happy should not be confined to the realms of our job roles or titles but should extend into the values, activities, and relationships that give our lives meaning.

Engaging in this introspection might reveal that happiness at work isn't solely about the tasks we perform but about the environment, the culture, the people, and the sense of achievement we derive from our roles. It might be the autonomy in decision-making, the opportunities for growth, the meaningfulness of the work, or the company's values that align with our own. It's imperative to break down these elements to understand their weight in our professional satisfaction.

One key aspect to consider is the role of challenges and accomplishments. Often, happiness is intertwined with the feeling of progress and achievement. Identifying the projects or tasks that make us feel most accomplished can provide valuable insights into what makes us genuinely happy at work. It's not just about the end goal but about the process, the learning curve, and the resilience built along the way.

Another area to reflect upon is the balance between our personal and professional lives. How does this balance—or the lack thereof—affect our happiness? It's essential to consider how our work integrates with or disrupts other areas of our life, as true happiness cannot thrive in an environment where one aspect consistently overshadows or undermines another.

Communication and relationships at work also play a crucial role in shaping our happiness. The rapport we share with our colleagues, the support system within our workspace, and how acknowledged and appreciated we feel, contribute significantly to feeling joyful and motivated. Evaluating these aspects can shed light on changes that might enhance our work experience.

The physical and mental challenges of our jobs are noteworthy considerations as well. How does our role impact our physical health and mental well-being? Jobs that align with our physical capabilities and mental health needs are more likely to foster happiness. Identifying any misalignments in this area is crucial for making informed decisions about our career paths.

Aside from introspection, seeking feedback can be instrumental in identifying what makes us happy. Sometimes, an external perspective can highlight strengths and passions we might overlook. This feedback, combined with our self-reflection, can form a clearer picture of where our joy truly lies within our professional lives.

One cannot overlook the significance of aligning our job roles with our core values and purpose. Understanding what we stand for and seeking roles that allow us to express and live by those values can immensely contribute to our happiness at work. It's about finding synergy between who we are and what we do.

In this personal journey, experimenting and exploring new roles, responsibilities, and even new career paths can be enlightening. Sometimes, stepping out of our comfort zones reveals what truly makes us happy, what challenges us in the right ways, and what contributes to our growth and satisfaction.

Moreover, recognizing the impermanence and evolution of happiness is vital. What makes us happy today may not hold the same value tomorrow. Our professional and personal growth brings new perspectives, altering our definition of happiness. Embracing this fluidity allows us to adapt and find joy in different stages of our career and life.

In practical terms, creating a 'happiness map' can be a helpful tool. This involves documenting the moments, tasks, and interactions that bring us joy at work. Over time, this map can serve as a guide to making career decisions that align with our sources of happiness.

Engaging in mindfulness and gratitude practices can enhance our awareness and appreciation of the moments of joy in our work life. By consciously acknowledging these moments, we wire our brains to recognize and seek out what makes us happy. This positive reinforcement loop not only uplifts our mood but gradually steers our career trajectory towards more fulfilling paths.

As we delve deeper into the pathways to happiness at work, understanding and identifying what makes us genuinely happy is the foundation upon which we can build a fulfilling professional life. This self-knowledge empowers us to make informed decisions, advocate for our needs, and create a work environment that resonates with our deepest desires for joy, growth, and satisfaction.

Ultimately, happiness at work is deeply personal and subjective. While the path to discovering it is unique for each individual, the journey itself offers valuable insights into our character, aspirations, and what truly matters to us. Embracing this journey with openness, curiosity, and intention holds the key to unlocking our happiness at work and, by extension, in our lives.

Seeking Job Satisfaction and Fulfillment

When we look at our work lives, seeking job satisfaction and fulfillment isn't just a luxury—it's a necessity for our overall well-being. We spend a significant part of our lives at work, so it's only natural that we strive to find happiness and fulfillment in what we do. But how do we embark on this journey? How do we uncover what truly satisfies us and ensures our days are more than just a countdown to the weekend?

The first step in seeking job satisfaction is to understand what it means to you personally. Satisfaction at work can come from various sources—achievement, recognition, a sense of purpose, or the relationships we build with our coworkers. It's essential to reflect on which aspects of your work life bring you the most joy and satisfaction. By pinpointing these elements, you can start to craft a career that aligns more closely with your values and desires.

Understanding our strengths and passions plays a crucial role in this process. When we work in a role that taps into our strengths and allows us to do what we love, job satisfaction naturally follows. Take some time to assess your skills and interests. Ask yourself what tasks you look forward to and what projects energize you. This self-reflection is a powerful tool in steering your career towards greater fulfillment.

Setting clear career goals is another important factor. Goals give us something to strive for and help to map out a pathway to fulfillment. They can be stepping stones towards the larger vision we have for our career. However, it's crucial that these goals are aligned with your values and what you genuinely want from your work life, not just what you think you should be aiming for.

It's also beneficial to seek feedback from others. Sometimes, an outside perspective can offer invaluable insights into our strengths and areas for growth. Engage in conversations with your colleagues, managers, or mentors about your performance and where you could shine within your role or organization. This feedback can inform your journey toward a more satisfying work life.

Finding fulfilment also means being proactive about the opportunities we pursue. Don't wait for chances to come to you; seek them out. Whether it's volunteering for a new project, seeking additional training, or proposing innovative ideas to your team, taking initiative can lead to more engaging and fulfilling work experiences.

Adaptability is a key trait in this pursuit. The world of work is constantly changing, and our ability to adapt to new roles, responsibilities, or environments can greatly influence our satisfaction. View each change as an opportunity to learn and grow, rather than a hurdle. This mindset shift can make all the difference in finding fulfillment in your career.

The importance of workplace relationships should not be underestimated. Strong connections with colleagues create a supportive and enjoyable work environment. Invest time in building these relationships. Whether it's through collaborative projects or social events, fostering a sense of community at work can enhance your job satisfaction dramatically.

Balancing work and life is also crucial for fulfillment. Ensure that you're making time for the people and activities that matter most to you outside of work. This balance helps prevent burnout and keeps you motivated and happy in your role. It's about finding harmony between your professional and personal lives, allowing each to enrich the other.

Don't forget to celebrate your successes, no matter how small. Recognizing your achievements can boost your morale and motivation. Celebrating these moments encourages a positive outlook on your work and career, contributing to overall job satisfaction.

If, after your best efforts, you find that your current role or employer isn't aligned with your pursuit of satisfaction and fulfillment, it may be time to reconsider your career path. It's okay to make changes and seek environments that better suit your needs and aspirations. Sometimes, the path to fulfillment involves making tough decisions about our current work situations.

Maintain a learner's mindset. Be open to new experiences and continuous learning. The more you're willing to grow and evolve in your career, the more satisfied you're likely to be. Every new skill or piece of knowledge is a step toward a more fulfilling work life.

It's important to practice gratitude. Focusing on the aspects of your job that you're thankful for can transform your outlook on work. Even in challenging times, recognizing the positives can foster resilience and satisfaction.

Seeking job satisfaction and fulfillment is a multifaceted journey that requires self-reflection, clarity, goal-setting, and a proactive and adaptable approach. By understanding what fulfillment means to you and actively pursuing it, you can transform your work life into a source of joy and satisfaction. Remember, the pathway to fulfillment is as unique as you are—embrace your journey with open arms and an open heart.

Rethinking Your Job and Its Role in Your Life

It's all too easy to fall into the trap of viewing our jobs purely as a means to an end. We wake up, clock in, perform our duties, and clock out - often without taking a moment to reflect on the impact our work has on our lives beyond the paycheck. This section is about challenging that perspective and delving deeper into understanding the role our jobs play in our overall happiness and well-being.

First and foremost, it's vital to recognize that our careers can be a significant source of fulfillment and joy. They provide us with challenges that stimulate our minds, opportunities to connect with others, and the chance to contribute to something larger than ourselves. When we start to see our jobs through this lens, the daily grind can transform into a fulfilling journey. But how do we start rethinking our jobs in this way?

The journey begins with introspection. Ask yourself: What aspects of my job do I truly enjoy? It could be the creative problem-solving, the interaction with clients, or perhaps the sense of accomplishment from completing a project. Identifying these elements not only boosts our appreciation for our work but also opens the door to seeking out more of what makes us happy on the job.

Of course, not every aspect of our jobs will spark joy - and that's okay. The key is to find a balance. When the less enjoyable tasks begin to outweigh the rewarding ones, it might be time to initiate a conversation with your manager about reshaping your role. This can lead to increased job satisfaction and a deeper sense of purpose in your work.

Another crucial component is setting clear boundaries between work and personal life. In today's digital age, it's easier than ever to bring work home with us. By establishing firm boundaries, like designating off-limits times for work emails, we safeguard our personal time for relaxation and rejuvenation. This balance is essential for maintaining a healthy perspective on our jobs and their place in our lives.

Embracing lifelong learning is also transformative. When we commit to continually developing new skills and knowledge, our careers can adapt and grow with us. This approach keeps us engaged and excited about the future, regardless of the inevitable industry shifts or changes in job roles.

It's also important to remember the value of relationships in rethinking our jobs. The connections we build at work can provide a profound sense of belonging and community. Cherishing these relationships makes our workdays more enjoyable and fulfilling, which in turn enhances our overall productivity and job satisfaction.

Seeking feedback is another powerful tool. Constructive criticism can not only improve our job performance but also help us feel more invested in our work. By actively seeking out opportunities for growth and improvement, we demonstrate a commitment to excellence that can redefine our roles for the better.

One of the most empowering steps we can take is to align our jobs with our personal values. When our work reflects what we care about most, it ceases to be just a job and becomes a meaningful part of our lives. This alignment can significantly boost our motivation and contentment at work.

Visualizing our career path plays a crucial role as well. Setting long-term goals and understanding how our current role fits into that trajectory can infuse our daily tasks with purpose. This long-term perspective can help us navigate difficult periods, knowing they are stepping stones to our larger aspirations.

It's also beneficial to foster a mindset of gratitude. Recognizing and appreciating the opportunities our jobs provide can make a significant difference in how we perceive our work. A simple shift in focus from what's lacking to what's available to us can transform our job into a more satisfying endeavor.

Cultivating resilience is essential in rethinking our jobs. Every job has its ups and downs, but viewing challenges as opportunities for growth rather than insurmountable obstacles can make all the difference. This resilience ensures we stay engaged and positive, even when the going gets tough.

Don't shy away from seeking out mentorship or support. Connecting with someone who has navigated their own career challenges can provide invaluable insights and encouragement. It's a powerful reminder that we're not alone in our journey and that growth often comes from the most unexpected places.

It's important to remember that rethinking our jobs is a continuous process. Our interests, goals, and life circumstances will evolve over time, and so too should our approach to our work. By staying flexible and open-minded, we ensure that our jobs continue to fulfill us at every stage of our careers.

Rethinking our jobs and their role in our lives offers a pathway to greater happiness and fulfillment at work. Through introspection, boundary setting, and a commitment to growth, we can transform our careers into a source of joy and meaning. It's not just about what we do from nine to five, but how we integrate our work into a fulfilling life narrative. Embrace the journey, and watch as your job becomes more than just a job, but a integral part of your pathway to happiness.

Chapter 5:
Staying Motivated
Throughout the Week

Maintaining motivation after conquering Monday might seem like a Herculean task as the week stretches out before us, filled with obligations, deadlines, and often unforeseen challenges. Yet, it's the fuel that keeps our engine running, steering us towards not just surviving but thriving in our personal and professional lives. Key to this endeavor is remembering your purpose. It's easy to get bogged down in the details of daily tasks and forget the bigger picture, the why behind the what. Every task, no matter how small it seems, contributes to this larger purpose. Keeping this in mind can transform mundane activities into pieces of a larger, fulfilling puzzle, making it easier to stay motivated and push through the toughest days.

Seeking continuous improvement involves a mindset that views challenges as opportunities to learn and grow rather than insurmountable obstacles. This mindset shift can make all the difference. It's about setting your sights on progress, not perfection. By focusing on making incremental changes and celebrating small victories along the way, you build a positive feedback loop that energizes and motivates you throughout the week. It's a journey of becoming, where each step, no matter how small, is a step towards a better version of yourself. This pursuit of excellence keeps the spark of motivation alive, turning what could be a struggle through the week into an exciting adventure of self-discovery and improvement.

Maintaining momentum after Monday requires a strategic approach to your week. It involves planning and foresight—anticipating potential pitfalls and preparing for them. It's about managing your energy as much as managing your time. Recognizing that your energy levels will fluctuate provides an opportunity to match high-priority tasks with high-energy moments. Equally important is recognizing the need for rest and recuperation, allowing yourself moments within the week to recharge. By managing your week this way, you ensure that motivation is not just a start-of-the-week phenomenon but a constant companion, helping you navigate through each day with purpose, progress, and vitality.

Remembering Your Purpose

As we dive into this crucial part of maintaining motivation throughout the week, it's essential to focus on the compass that guides us: our purpose. Knowing why we do what we do provides us with the fuel to keep our engines running, even when the road gets rough.

For many of us, our jobs are more than just a paycheck. They're a reflection of our passions, skills, and the impact we hope to make in the world. Yet, amidst the hustle and bustle of daily tasks and deadlines, it's easy to lose sight of this bigger picture. That's why actively remembering our purpose is not just beneficial; it's necessary.

Consider your role at work. It could be helping people, creating something new, solving problems, or making processes more efficient. Whatever it is, take a moment to reflect on how your role contributes to a greater good. This sense of contribution is a powerful motivator that can turn mundane tasks into pieces of a larger, fulfilling puzzle.

But, how do we keep our purpose at the forefront of our minds, especially when Monday blues or midweek slumps hit? One effective strategy is starting each day with a reminder. This could be a note to yourself, a motivational quote related to your goals, or a few minutes of reflection on what you're grateful for in your work. These small practices can make a significant impact on your attitude and approach to your day.

Visual reminders can also play a crucial role. Whether it's a photo that reminds you of why you chose your career or a vision board that captures your professional goals, having something tangible to look at can help reignite your passion.

Another key aspect is connecting with the impact of your work. If possible, get feedback from those who benefit directly from your efforts. Understanding how your work improves lives or contributes to the greater good can be incredibly inspiring and reaffirming.

Goal setting is another powerful technique. By setting specific, achievable goals that are aligned with your purpose, you create a roadmap that not only guides you but also motivates you. Celebrating small victories along the way fuels your drive and keeps the flame of purpose alive.

Mentorship can also be invaluable. Mentors can help you navigate challenges, offer perspective, and remind you of your strengths and the value of your contributions. Their belief in your potential can be a potent source of motivation.

Sharing your experiences and aspirations with colleagues or loved ones can also reinforce your commitment to your purpose. Talking about your goals and the reasons behind them can help solidify them in your mind and might even inspire others.

Furthermore, it's crucial to regularly reassess and realign your actions with your purpose. Our goals and passions can evolve, and so can the pathways to achieving them. Regularly taking stock of where you are in relation to where you want to be can help ensure that your daily work aligns with your long-term aspirations.

When setbacks occur, view them as opportunities to learn rather than insurmountable obstacles. Challenges can clarify our purpose, test our resilience, and ultimately, contribute to personal growth and fulfillment.

In the pursuit of our purpose, it's important to nurture our well-being. Ensuring adequate rest, engaging in activities we love outside of work, and maintaining healthy relationships enable us to show up fully and passionately in our professional lives.

Practice patience and persistence. Realizing our purpose is a journey, not a destination. It requires time, effort, and dedication. The road may be long and winding, but remembering why we embarked on it in the first place can make all the difference.

By weaving these strategies into the fabric of our daily lives, remembering our purpose becomes more than an exercise; it becomes a way of living. A purpose-driven life infuses each workday with significance, transforming even the most challenging Mondays into opportunities to contribute, learn, and grow.

So, let's embrace our purpose, allowing it to guide us through the highs and lows, knowing that it's not just about enduring another week but about moving closer to the meaningful goals that fuel our passion and perseverance.

Seeking Continuous Improvement

One of the cornerstones of staying motivated throughout the week is the commitment to continuous improvement. It's not just about getting through Monday or making it to Friday. It's about fostering a mindset that looks for opportunities to grow, learn, and become more effective in both our professional and personal lives. This approach isn't just a strategy; it's a way of life that transcends the typical ebb and flow of workweek emotions.

Continuous improvement involves setting personal benchmarks and systematically working to surpass them. This means celebrating each victory, no matter how small, and using it as a foundation for future successes. At times, this process will involve self-reflection and the honest appraisal of where we stand versus where we aspire to be.

Keeping a journal of accomplishments and areas for growth can significantly aid this journey. By documenting our progress, we can see how far we've come and what areas require additional attention. This practice can also serve as a reminder of our capability to overcome challenges and adapt to change, which in itself is a powerful motivator.

Seeking feedback from colleagues and supervisors can also propel us toward our goals. Constructive criticism is invaluable for identifying blind spots in our performance or behavior that we might not see ourselves. Embracing such feedback with grace and a genuine desire to improve can lead to significant growth and development.

Another facet of continuous improvement is lifelong learning. Our quest for knowledge should never stagnate. Whether it's by taking up new courses related to our field, engaging in seminars, or simply dedicating time to read, we nourish our minds and continually add to our skill sets. This not only makes our work more engaging but also keeps us competitive and relevant in our industries.

Setting incremental goals is paramount. By breaking down larger objectives into smaller, manageable tasks, we can maintain a sense of progress and accomplishment. This method prevents us from feeling overwhelmed, keeps us focused, and ensures that we're always moving in the right direction.

Innovation plays a key role in continuous improvement. This means being open to new ideas, methodologies, and technologies that can revolutionize our approach to work. It's about challenging the status quo and being a catalyst for change, not only in our tasks but also in our environment. Encouraging innovation not only fosters personal growth but also contributes to creating a dynamic and forward-thinking workplace culture.

It's crucial to maintain a balance between work and personal life in this pursuit. Continuous improvement should enhance our lives, not lead to burnout. Taking time for rest and recovery is just as important as pushing the boundaries of what we can achieve. It allows us to return to our tasks with a renewed focus and energy, ready to tackle new challenges.

Promoting a culture of continuous improvement within a team or organization can have a transformative effect. When everyone is engaged in bettering themselves and the collective, it creates a vibrant, supportive, and highly motivated environment. This culture not only elevates performance but also strengthens interpersonal relationships and job satisfaction.

Understanding our intrinsic motivations is crucial to this journey. Knowing what drives us, whether it be personal satisfaction, recognition, or the desire to contribute to something larger, can help align our efforts with our values and goals. This alignment ensures that our pursuit of continuous improvement is both meaningful and fulfilling.

Often, the biggest obstacle in continuous improvement is the fear of failure. It's important to recognize that growth inherently involves setbacks and challenges. Viewing these experiences not as failures but as learning opportunities is vital. This perspective encourages resilience and the understanding that every effort leads us closer to our goals, even when the path isn't linear.

To truly excel, it's essential to practice self-compassion. Being overly critical can hinder our progress. Instead, acknowledging our efforts and forgiving ourselves for any shortcomings allows us to move forward with confidence and determination.

Maintaining momentum after Monday, as we'll explore further, is about implementing these strategies consistently, not just when motivation is high. Continuous improvement is a marathon, not a sprint. It requires dedication, patience, and above all, a commitment to the process.

Fostering an environment that supports continuous improvement is invaluable. This includes creating spaces for collaboration, encouraging open communication, and ensuring that resources are available for personal and professional development. By investing in an ecosystem that nurtures growth, we set ourselves and those around us up for lasting success and satisfaction.

Seeking continuous improvement is a multifaceted endeavor that touches on all aspects of our lives. It's a journey marked by successes, learning moments, and a relentless pursuit of excellence. By embracing this path, we not only enhance our own lives but also make a positive impact on our workplaces and communities. The goal is to make every week better than the last, turning each challenge into an opportunity for growth and each day into a step toward our ultimate objectives.

Maintaining Momentum After Monday

The challenge doesn't end when you conquer Monday. In fact, it's just the beginning of a perpetual cycle of maintaining that hard-won momentum throughout the rest of the week. This narrative shift is essential; thinking beyond the initial victory allows us to frame each week as an opportunity for continuous success and satisfaction.

First, it's critical to recognize the psychological shift that occurs after Monday. The initial adrenaline of starting a new week fades away, leaving room for the mid-week slump if we're not careful. To mitigate this, keep your purpose at the forefront of your mind. Reminding yourself why the work you do matters can help maintain a high level of motivation even as the week progresses.

Fostering a mindset of continuous improvement is another pivotal strategy in keeping the momentum alive. Each day presents an opportunity to reflect on what went well and where there's room for improvement. This mindset ensures that even the smallest victories are celebrated and the lessons are integrated, making the following day even more productive.

Another technique involves breaking the week into manageable chunks. Rather than viewing the week as one big block, break it down into days or even specific tasks. This helps in maintaining focus and reducing the feeling of being overwhelmed, making each task seem more approachable.

Setting micro-goals for each day is a great way to keep the momentum going. These should be specific, measurable, achievable, relevant, and time-bound (S-M-A-R-T) goals that will help inch you closer to your broader objectives. Achieving these smaller goals provides a sense of accomplishment that fuels further motivation.

It's also beneficial to incorporate regular reviews of your progress throughout the week. This could be a brief reflection at the end of each day or a more formal review at mid-week. Understanding your progress helps in adjusting strategies and staying aligned with your objectives.

Engage in team huddles or check-ins with colleagues if you work in a collaborative environment. These interactions not only build a supportive community but also serve as accountability mechanisms, keeping everyone motivated and focused on common goals.

Don't underestimate the power of maintaining a positive attitude. It's easy to get bogged down by setbacks or challenges, but staying optimistic and resilient can significantly impact your ability and willingness to push forward.

Keeping your workspace organized and clutter-free also contributes significantly to maintaining momentum. A tidy space can enhance focus and productivity, reducing the mental load and increasing efficiency.

Incorporating variety into your workweek is another effective strategy. Monotony is the enemy of motivation. By varying your tasks, incorporating new methods, or even changing your environment, you can keep your engagement levels high.

Remember the importance of self-care throughout the week. Little acts of kindness towards yourself, like healthy eating, adequate rest, and physical activity, can dramatically affect your energy levels and general well-being, sustaining your momentum.

Being flexible and adaptable to changes can also positively impact your ability to maintain momentum. Accept that not everything will go as planned and that agility in response to unforeseen changes can keep you moving forward.

Celebrate the week's end as a milestone, not just a relief from work. Recognizing the effort you've put in and the progress you've made provides a psychological reset that prepares you for the upcoming week with a fresh perspective and renewed energy.

Maintaining momentum after Monday requires a combination of strategic planning, positive mindset, and continuous personal growth. It's about finding joy in the journey, celebrating the small victories, and pushing through the challenges with resilience and determination. By adopting these practices, you can transform the entire week into a series of opportunities for success and satisfaction.

To sum up, staying motivated throughout the week is a multifaceted endeavor that requires intentional actions, reflections, and mindset shifts. It's about more than just surviving the post-Monday world; it's about thriving in it, harnessing the initial push of the week, and riding that wave all the way to Friday. By intentionally focusing on maintaining momentum, we set ourselves up for a rewarding and productive week, laying the foundation for long-term success and well-being.

Chapter 6:
Employers' Role in Mitigating Monday Blues

As we pivot from looking inward and addressing personal strategies to combat Monday Blues, it's crucial to zoom out and examine the pivotal role employers play in this equation. The start of the workweek doesn't have to be a dread-filled descent but can instead signal a beginning filled with potential and positivity. A significant portion of this shift hinges on workplace practices and culture, particularly how employers address work-life balance and employee well-being.

Employers, perhaps without even realizing it, hold the torch when it comes to setting the tone for the week ahead. Encouraging work/life balance isn't just about allowing employees to leave early or work from home; it's about valuing their need to recharge, to spend time with family, or to pursue personal projects. This respect for personal time directly combats the encroaching dread of Monday, empowering employees to feel more balanced and fulfilled.

Increasing flexibility and accommodations in the workplace can take many forms, from adjustable work hours to recognizing and supporting varied work styles. Such measures reflect an understanding that productivity is not a one-size-fits-all scenario and acknowledging this can greatly diminish the Sunday night anxiety about the impending week. Empowering employees to adjust their schedules to better fit their personal lives can dramatically decrease stress and improve morale.

Granting more vacation time can also be a game-changer. It signals to employees that their well-being is a priority and that taking time off to rejuvenate is not only accepted but encouraged. This can lead to a more refreshed and energized start to the week when they return, with the Monday Blues barely making a ripple in their enthusiasm.

Fair compensation is another crucial piece of this puzzle. Feeling undervalued is a significant contributor to job dissatisfaction, which can exacerbate the Monday Blues. Ensuring employees feel fairly compensated for their work contributes to a sense of value and appreciation, which can motivate a more positive start to the week.

In addition, reducing Monday meetings can offer employees a softer start to the week. Instead of diving straight into a structured, often stressful environment, employees can ease into their work, prioritize their tasks, and mentally prepare for the week ahead. This can significantly cut down on the Sunday night dread and the Monday morning scramble.

Engaging in positive communication sets a powerful precedent for the week. When leaders start Monday with positive affirmations, acknowledge team achievements, and communicate constructively, it breeds a culture of positivity that can make Mondays much more palatable.

Providing incentives and appreciation for Monday achievements can also shift the day's dynamic. Whether it's recognizing the completion of tasks, celebrating milestones, or simply acknowledging the effort it takes to switch back into work mode, these gestures can transform how employees view the start of the week.

Implementing self-care perks, such as providing healthy snacks, yoga classes, or meditation sessions, can also play a significant role. These gestures show a commitment to employee well-being that extends beyond professional achievements and into holistic health.

Finally, creating a supportive work environment is perhaps the most significant action employers can take. When employees feel supported, respected, and valued, Monday becomes less of a hurdle and more of a welcome opportunity. It's about building a culture where employees feel their well-being is prioritized, their work is meaningful, and their contributions are recognized. In such a setting, the Monday Blues don't stand a chance.

Encouraging Work/Life Balance

One of the most effective strategies for mitigating Monday blues lies in the hands of employers: encouraging a healthy work/life balance. In today's fast-paced work environment, the line between personal and professional lives can blur, making it crucial for employers to actively promote a culture where balance is not only encouraged but practiced. It's about recognizing employees as humans first, who have lives, responsibilities, and interests outside of work that are equally important.

Creating a work environment that values work/life balance starts with understanding. Understanding that when employees feel overwhelmed, their job performance and personal life suffer. It's a chain reaction that affects the overall morale of the workplace. Employers have the power to create an atmosphere that fosters productivity during work hours, allowing employees to fully enjoy their time off without worries or work-related stress hanging over their heads.

One tangible way to promote this balance is through flexible scheduling. This means allowing employees to shift their start and end times, or even work from home on occasion. Such policies acknowledge that employees have varying peak productivity periods and personal commitments that might not align with a traditional 9-to-5 schedule. This flexibility can lead to a more engaged and satisfied workforce, as it shows trust and respect for the employee's ability to manage their time effectively.

Addressing the issue of constant connectivity is another crucial aspect. In an age where technology keeps us tethered to work 24/7, it's vital for employers to set clear boundaries. Encouraging employees to disconnect outside of work hours, emphasizing that emails and messages sent after hours can wait until the next business day, can significantly reduce burnout and stress, contributing to a healthier work/life balance.

Incorporating mental health days into the benefits package is also a progressive step towards acknowledging the importance of work/life balance. Mental health days are paid leave days specifically set aside for employees to take a break when they are feeling overwhelmed or burned out. This acknowledges mental health as a priority and a critical component of employees' overall well-being.

Recognition of the importance of personal time can also extend to how tasks and projects are assigned. Employers should ensure that workloads are realistic and that deadlines are set with an understanding of employees' capacities and other commitments. Overworking employees can lead to burnout and resentment, which are counterproductive to fostering a motivated and productive workforce.

Encouraging vacations and time off is equally important. Employers should create an environment where taking time off is not only allowed but encouraged. Employees should feel comfortable taking their allocated vacation time without fear of repercussions or the dread of coming back to an overwhelming workload. It's about promoting the idea that time off is part of the work cycle - a period for rest and recharge that ultimately benefits both the employee and the company.

Another approach is promoting well-being through work-sponsored activities or initiatives that focus on physical health, mental well-being, and social connections. Whether it's through offering gym memberships, hosting mindfulness sessions, or organizing team outings, these activities can significantly contribute to an employee's sense of well-being, and in turn, a better work/life balance.

At the heart of fostering work/life balance is communication. Open lines of communication where employees feel comfortable discussing their work/life balance with their managers can make a big difference. This can involve regular check-ins or feedback sessions where employees can voice their concerns or suggestions related to workload, work arrangements, and overall well-being.

Leadership training that emphasizes empathy and understanding is crucial. Managers and leaders should be equipped with the skills to recognize signs of burnout or stress in their teams and to respond with supportive measures. Leadership plays a pivotal role in setting the tone and culture of the workplace when it comes to work/life balance.

Furthermore, celebrating achievements and milestones, both professional and personal, reinforces the value placed on employees' lives outside of work. Recognizing an employee's work anniversary, birthdays, or personal milestones like weddings or the birth of a child fosters a sense of belonging and appreciation that transcends the professional realm.

Leading by example is perhaps the most powerful tool in encouraging work/life balance. When senior leaders and managers practice and prioritize work/life balance in their own lives, it sends a clear message to the rest of the company that it's a core value of the organization. It's about walking the talk and showing that it's possible to have a thriving career while also maintaining a fulfilling personal life.

Encouraging work/life balance is a multifaceted challenge that requires a holistic approach. It's about creating a workplace culture that recognizes and supports the notion that employees are at their best when there is harmony between their professional and personal lives. Employers who take active steps to promote and enforce policies that support a healthy work/life balance will not only mitigate the dreaded Monday blues but will also cultivate a workforce that is engaged, motivated, and loyal. It's a win-win scenario where both the company and its employees thrive together, fostering a positive work environment that stands the test of time.

By integrating these practices, organizations can make significant strides in reducing the prevalence of Monday blues and, in turn, enhance the overall job satisfaction and well-being of their employees. It's not just about preventing the negatives associated with the start of the workweek but about creating a sustainable work-life paradigm that champions productivity, happiness, and health in equal measure.

Increasing Flexibility and Accommodations

The Monday Blues aren't an insurmountable force of nature, despite how they might feel at the start of each workweek. In contrast, employers hold significant power in shaping the work environment to mitigate these blues, particularly through increasing flexibility and accommodations. Creating a workplace that acknowledges and adapts to the diverse needs of its employees can transform Mondays from a day of dread to one of opportunity and positivity.

At the heart of increasing workplace flexibility and accommodations is the recognition of individuality. Every employee has unique circumstances, responsibilities, and challenges that affect their work-life balance. By offering flexible working hours, employers can cater to these individual needs, allowing employees to avoid rush-hour commutes, manage childcare responsibilities, or simply work when they feel most productive.

Remote work has emerged as a powerful tool in this arena. The capability to work from home – or any location with internet connectivity – can drastically reduce the anxiety and stress associated with commuting and office environments. This not only helps in combating the Monday Blues but also contributes to an overall increase in job satisfaction and employee well-being.

Job-sharing arrangements and part-time working opportunities further augment employer flexibility. Such arrangements can be particularly beneficial for employees going through life changes, pursuing further education, or dealing with health issues. By accommodating these needs, employers demonstrate a commitment to employee well-being, which in turn fosters loyalty and motivation.

Another aspect of increasing flexibility and accommodations involves rethinking meeting schedules. By avoiding scheduling meetings first thing on Monday morning, employers can give employees the much-needed space to ease into the week, prioritize their tasks, and set a positive tone for the days ahead.

It's also crucial for employers to recognize the importance of mental health days. Encouraging employees to take days off when they're feeling overwhelmed or stressed without penalizing them fosters an environment of trust and care. It's an implicit acknowledgment that mental health is just as important as physical health.

Customized workspace accommodations can play a significant role in mitigating Monday Blues. Whether it's allowing personalized workspaces, providing noise-cancelling headphones, or ensuring access to natural light, simple changes can make a significant difference in employee mood and productivity.

Providing employees with options for professional and personal development can also increase job satisfaction and engagement. When employees feel like they're growing and learning, Mondays can symbolize a fresh start and an opportunity to tackle new challenges.

Implementing a results-only work environment (ROWE) is another innovative approach. In a ROWE, employees are evaluated based on output rather than the number of hours worked. This shifts the focus from face-time to actual results, allowing employees the flexibility to work in a way that suits them best.

The role of transparent communication in facilitating flexibility and accommodations cannot be overstated. Employers should ensure that policies are communicated clearly and that employees feel comfortable discussing their needs without fear of judgment or repercussions.

Feedback loops are essential in fine-tuning policies and practices related to flexibility and accommodations. Regular check-ins with employees can help employers understand what's working and what isn't, leading to continuous improvement and adaptation.

Leadership training on the importance of flexibility and accommodations can equip managers with the skills and empathy needed to support their teams effectively. Leaders play a pivotal role in setting the tone and culture of the workplace, and their support is crucial in mitigating the Monday Blues.

Ultimately, increasing flexibility and accommodations is about creating a culture of support and understanding within the workplace. It's about recognizing that when employees feel supported, they're more engaged, productive, and happier. This not only benefits employees but also contributes to the overall success of the organization.

The fight against the Monday Blues is multifaceted, requiring commitment and creativity from employers. Through thoughtful policies and a genuine concern for employee well-being, Mondays can transform from a day of dread to a day of excitement and potential. This doesn't just benefit employees; it's a win-win for organizations striving for productivity, innovation, and a positive workplace culture.

The journey towards mitigating Monday Blues through increased flexibility and accommodations is ongoing. It's an evolution in workplace culture that reflects a deeper understanding of human psychology and the diverse needs of the modern workforce. By embracing this approach, employers can lead the way in creating workplaces that not only mitigate the Monday Blues but also foster a thriving, engaged, and satisfied workforce.

Allowing More Vacation Time

In the ongoing quest to beat the Monday blues, one strategy stands out for its simplicity and transformative potential: allowing more vacation time. Vacation isn't just a luxury; it's a crucial component of a healthy work-life balance, providing employees the time they need to rest, rejuvenate, and return to their jobs with renewed energy and perspective.

Imagine starting your week, not with dread, but with stories of adventure, relaxation, or quality time spent with loved ones. This isn't just a fantasy—it's a real possibility when employers recognize the value of vacation time. It's about shifting the mindset from seeing time off as time lost to seeing it as an investment in employee well-being and productivity.

The benefits of vacation extend far beyond the individual. They ripple through the entire workplace, leading to a brighter, more motivated team. When employees get adequate downtime, they're not the only ones who benefit—their renewed vigor and fresh ideas often lead to better problem-solving and creativity, directly benefiting the employer.

However, it's essential to acknowledge that merely allocating more vacation time isn't enough. It's about creating a culture where taking time off is encouraged and celebrated, not frowned upon or met with behind-the-scenes grumbling. It's where leadership plays a pivotal role, setting the tone by utilizing their vacation time and openly discussing the positive impact it's had on their work and personal life.

Think about the message it sends when a manager or CEO openly talks about their vacation experiences and encourages others to take their deserved time off. It underlines the company's commitment to work-life balance and illustrates a deep understanding that to bring your best self to work, stepping away is not only beneficial, it's necessary.

To implement this change, companies need to review and possibly overhaul their vacation policies, ensuring they're not just offering more time off but making it accessible. This means simplifying the process of requesting vacation, ensuring adequate coverage, and discouraging the stockpiling of vacation days without using them.

Encouraging employees to take time off can also involve creative solutions, such as vacation stipends, planned company-wide days off, or even rewarding top performers with additional vacation days. These strategies not only promote the use of vacation time but also show appreciation for employees' hard work.

It's also crucial to address a common fear among employees: the worry of returning to an overwhelming workload. This can be mitigated by encouraging and even training staff to handle some of their colleagues' tasks during their absence, ensuring a smoother transition back to work for the vacationing employee.

Feedback loops can play an essential role, too. By soliciting and acting on employee input on vacation policies and their impact, companies can continuously improve their approaches. This feedback can highlight unforeseen challenges and provide insights into further enhancing the workplace atmosphere.

The result of allowing more vacation time can be profound. Employees return to work feeling appreciated and rejuvenated, which translates into higher quality work, increased engagement, and a more harmonious workplace culture. In turn, this positive atmosphere can significantly reduce the Monday blues, as employees have both the time to recharge and the knowledge that their well-being is a priority.

But the benefits don't stop there. In the bigger picture, companies that are generous with vacation time often find themselves at the top of the list of desirable places to work, attracting and retaining top talent. This is more important than ever in today's competitive job market, where the best employees are not just looking for a job, but a place where their contributions are valued and their well-being is prioritized.

Allowing more vacation time is more than just a perk—it's a strategic move that acknowledges the human element of work. It's a statement that a company understands life's demands and is committed to providing its employees with the time they need to meet those demands, enjoy their lives, and return to their jobs with enthusiasm. Beating the Monday blues, therefore, starts with recognizing that time off is not an enemy of productivity, but one of its greatest allies.

As we continue to navigate the complexities of the modern workplace, let's not underestimate the power of vacation. It's not just about taking a break from work; it's about creating a work environment that respects, nurtures, and values its members. The path to a happier, more productive workplace and the mitigation of Monday blues may very well start with the simple act of allowing more vacation time.

Fair Compensation for Employees

Navigating the intricate world of employee satisfaction and engagement reveals a multifaceted approach where fair compensation emerges as a critical cornerstone. It's undeniable that feeling valued and fairly compensated plays a vital role in mitigating the infamous Monday blues. This chapter delves deeper into the essence of fair compensation and its profound impact on employees' attitudes towards Mondays and their overall job satisfaction.

At the heart of fair compensation lies the principle of equity and recognition for one's contributions. A fair compensation package is not merely about meeting industry standards or benchmarks; it's about acknowledging the unique value each employee brings to the table. When employees perceive their compensation as equitable, they are more likely to feel respected and valued by their employer, which sets a positive tone for the week ahead.

Moreover, fair compensation extends beyond the paycheck. It encompasses benefits, bonuses, recognition programs, and opportunities for professional development. An approach that considers the holistic well-being of employees demonstrates an employer's commitment to their overall satisfaction and work-life harmony. This comprehensive view of compensation is crucial for starting the week on a positive note, with employees feeling supported both financially and professionally.

There's also an intrinsic link between fair compensation and motivation. When employees feel that their efforts are fairly rewarded, their drive to excel and contribute meaningfully increases. This motivation carries over from the energized buzz of Friday's achievements into a positive momentum on Monday morning, effectively countering the Monday blues.

Yet, it's important to recognize that perceptions of fairness are subjective and vary widely among individuals. Employers must therefore engage in open conversations about compensation, inviting feedback and providing transparency around compensation policies. Such dialogues can dispel doubts and build trust, ensuring that employees feel their contributions are fairly evaluated and rewarded.

In addressing fair compensation, employers also tackle job dissatisfaction head-on—one of the root causes of the Monday blues. By aligning compensation with performance, skill level, and market trends, employers can enhance job satisfaction, thereby making Mondays less daunting and more welcomed as a fresh start.

Furthermore, the act of reviewing and adjusting compensation packages regularly is a testament to an employer's dedication to fairness. This ongoing process reflects a dynamic approach to compensation that keeps pace with changes within the organization, industry, and broader economic landscape. Through this lens, Mondays can be seen as opportunities to strive for new heights, backed by an employer who values and supports their workforce.

Additionally, fair compensation plays a pivotal role in shaping the company culture. A culture that prioritizes fair and transparent compensation practices fosters a sense of belonging and community among employees. In such an environment, Mondays are no longer a hurdle but a harmonious return to a supportive and appreciative workspace.

For smaller businesses that might struggle with matching the compensation packages of larger corporations, emphasizing non-monetary forms of compensation can be equally effective. Flexible work arrangements, professional development opportunities, and a strong sense of community can all contribute to feelings of fair compensation. Such strategies can help alleviate the dread of Mondays by offering a work environment that values and nurtures its employees in a multitude of ways.

The positive ripple effects of fair compensation on an organization are significant. It not only enhances job satisfaction and motivation but also contributes to lower turnover rates. Employees who feel fairly compensated are more likely to stay with an organization, reducing the costs and disruptions associated with high turnover. This stability is beneficial for organizational growth and fosters a sense of familiarity and comfort that makes Mondays less intimidating.

It's also noteworthy that fair compensation practices contribute to equity and inclusivity in the workplace. By ensuring that compensation is based on objective criteria such as performance, experience, and job responsibilities, employers can mitigate biases that might otherwise exacerbate feelings of dissatisfaction and disenchantment, particularly on Mondays. This commitment to fairness and equity underscores the importance of starting each week on a positive, inclusive note.

Employers have a powerful tool at their disposal in the form of fair compensation to transform the dreaded Monday into an opportunity for growth and positivity. By embracing a comprehensive and equitable approach to compensation, organizations can foster a work environment where Mondays are approached with enthusiasm rather than anxiety.

The role of fair compensation in mitigating Monday blues cannot be overstated. It is a foundational element of employee satisfaction and motivation, directly influencing how employees perceive their value and contributions to the organization. Employers that prioritize fair compensation practices are not only investing in their employees' well-being but are also setting the stage for a more productive, engaged, and positive workforce. As we look towards creating workplaces that are vibrant and fulfilling, rethinking compensation is a critical step in the right direction.

By reconsidering and realigning compensation strategies, employers can effectively counteract the Monday blues, turning the start of the week into a launchpad for success and satisfaction. The pursuit of fair compensation is, therefore, not just a quest for equity but a strategic move towards cultivating a thriving workplace where every day, especially Monday, is welcomed with open arms and a ready spirit.

Reducing Monday Meetings

Let's dive straight into a challenge that faces many of us without even realizing its impact: the over-scheduling of Monday meetings. The dread of Monday morning is often amplified by a calendar bloated with meetings. From the moment employees clock in, they're thrust into back-to-back sessions, leaving little room for warm-up into the workweek or for tackling priority tasks.

Employers play a crucial role in mitigating this issue. The move towards reducing Monday meetings is not just about cutting down the number of meetings. It's about reassessing the necessity of meetings scheduled on a Monday and understanding how these meetings can shape the tone for the week ahead.

For starters, consider the purpose of these meetings. Are they truly urgent and necessary to kick-start the week, or can they be rescheduled to later in the week? This simple act of prioritization can alleviate the immediate pressure off employees' shoulders, offering them space to breathe and plan their week more effectively.

Moreover, transitioning some of these meetings to a written format, such as emails or shared documents, can retain the essence of communication without demanding synchronous attendance. This approach respects individual working styles and time management, catering to a more productive work environment.

Another strategy involves designated no-meeting days, with Monday being a prime candidate. This concept grants employees the autonomy to dive into deep work, critical thinking, and strategic planning without the interruption of meetings. It's a gesture that acknowledges the diversity in work dynamics and the need for uninterrupted focus, particularly at the beginning of the week.

On a similar note, when Monday meetings are unavoidable, it's imperative to make them as efficient as possible. This means setting clear agendas, sticking to scheduled time frames, and ensuring that only essential personnel are required to attend. These practices demonstrate respect for everyone's time and set a precedent for productivity and respect across the board.

Feedback loops are also vital. Employers should encourage open dialogue about meeting structures and their impact on employees' work and well-being. What works for one team may not work for another, and adaptability is key in finding a balanced approach that suits diverse needs.

Implementing meeting-free zones at the start and end of Mondays can offer a compromise — safeguarding time for focused work while still allowing for necessary team check-ins. It's about finding that sweet spot where communication remains fluid without overwhelming employees right out of the gate.

Technology can be a helpful ally in this mission. Leveraging collaborative tools and platforms can reduce the need for face-to-face meetings, enabling asynchronous communication and collaboration that respects individuals' workflow and time management preferences.

Leadership plays a pivotal role in modeling meeting etiquette. By demonstrating an understanding of the value of employees' time and a commitment to efficient meeting practices, leaders can set a positive example. This leadership approach encourages a culture where meetings are purposeful, concise, and impactful.

Moreover, introducing a Monday morning catch-up that's less formal and more about social connection can help ease employees into the week. A brief, optional gathering over coffee, for instance, can humanize the start of the week, building camaraderie and injecting a dose of motivation without the pressure of formal agenda items.

Encouraging focus on high-value activities at the beginning of the week can also shift the narrative around Mondays. When employees have the liberty to tackle meaningful, rewarding work first thing, it creates a momentum that carries throughout the week, aligning closely with intrinsic motivation and job satisfaction.

Adopting a flexible approach to Mondays — understanding that not every task needs to be initiated at the week's start — can alleviate the pressure that contributes to the Monday blues. This flexibility demonstrates trust in employees to manage their workload effectively, fostering a sense of autonomy and responsibility.

Reducing Monday meetings is more than a logistical adjustment; it's part of a broader strategy to enhance workplace well-being and productivity. By adopting these practices, employers can create an environment where Mondays are no longer synonymous with dread but are a launchpad for a fulfilling and productive week.

As we progress through this journey of transforming the workplace, it's clear that every action taken towards improving employees' morale and productivity has a ripple effect. The shift towards reducing Monday meetings is a testament to the power of thoughtful leadership and its impact on creating a positive, motivating work environment.

Engaging in Positive Communication

Communication is the heartbeat of any thriving workplace. When it comes to mitigating the pervasive Monday blues, the role of positive communication cannot be overstated. It's more than just exchanging information; it's about building relationships, fostering trust, and creating an environment where employees feel valued and understood. Engaging in positive communication is an art that requires mindfulness, empathy, and a genuine interest in the well-being of others.

One of the first steps in cultivating positive communication is active listening. It's easy to overlook, but its impact is profound. Active listening involves giving your full attention to the speaker, absorbing the message, and responding thoughtfully. It sends a powerful message of respect and validation, making employees feel heard and appreciated. This exchange fosters an atmosphere of mutual respect, which is essential for a healthy work environment.

Clarity is another cornerstone of positive communication. In a world where misinterpretation can lead to discontent or anxiety, being clear in expressing expectations, providing feedback, or conveying company goals can eliminate unnecessary confusion. It's important for employers to articulate their thoughts in a way that is direct yet considerate, reducing the room for misunderstanding and setting a positive tone for the workweek.

Positive reinforcement plays a pivotal role in shaping a workplace's culture. Recognizing and affirming employees' efforts and accomplishments not only boosts their morale but also motivates them to maintain or improve their performance. This practice should be consistent and genuine, ensuring that appreciation is directed at specific actions or achievements, making the feedback more meaningful.

Encouraging open dialogue is another vital aspect of positive communication. Creating channels for feedback, concerns, and suggestions signals to employees that their voices matter. It's essential to approach such exchanges with an open mind and a willingness to act on viable ideas and concerns. This openness not only enhances problem-solving and innovation but also strengthens the bond between employers and their workforce.

Empathy is the glue that holds positive communication together. Approaching conversations with an understanding of employees' perspectives and emotions can transform interactions. It involves acknowledging feelings, offering support, and sometimes, simply being there to listen. Empathy builds trust and loyalty, which are crucial for a motivated and engaged team.

Tackling difficult conversations with tact and sensitivity is equally important. Not every discussion will be comfortable, but how these conversations are handled can make a significant difference. Approaching sensitive topics with a positive intent, focusing on solutions rather than blame, and maintaining composure helps in navigating through challenging discussions while preserving dignity and respect.

The tone of communication also has a profound effect. The old adage, "It's not what you say, but how you say it," holds true. A positive, encouraging tone can uplift someone's spirits, whereas a negative tone can do the opposite. Awareness of one's tone, especially during stressful times, reflects emotional intelligence and a commitment to positive engagement.

Incorporating humor appropriately can lighten the mood and improve relationships. Laughter is a powerful tool for easing tension, building camaraderie, and fostering a positive work atmosphere. It's about finding joy in the day-to-day, making the workplace not just a place to work but also a place to find a sense of belonging and enjoyment.

Refraining from negative language and criticism that demeans or undermines individuals is critical. Constructive feedback is vital, but it should always aim to build up, not tear down. Offering solutions and support for improvement in a compassionate manner can turn potential negatives into opportunities for growth.

Maintaining consistency in communication is key to building trust. Inconsistencies between what is said and what is done can lead to skepticism and doubt. Being consistent means aligning actions with words, setting clear expectations, and following through on commitments. This reliability strengthens the foundation upon which positive communication is built.

Encouraging teamwork through positive communication not only enhances productivity but also fosters a sense of community. When team members communicate effectively, respect each other's opinions, and collaborate towards common goals, they create a supportive and dynamic work environment. This sense of unity is especially important in overcoming the collective dread of Mondays, as it reassures employees that they are part of a team that values their contribution.

Personalizing communication acknowledges the individuality of employees. People appreciate when they are seen as unique individuals rather than just part of a workforce. Tailoring communication to acknowledge someone's interests, strengths, and even challenges demonstrates care and attention, which can greatly boost morale and motivation.

Finally, encouraging a culture of gratitude within the workplace can transform the mood from dread to anticipation. Simple acts of gratitude, whether through a thank you note, a public acknowledgment, or a small token of appreciation, can have a lasting impact. It's about creating a culture where gratitude is not just an occasional gesture but a daily practice.

Engaging in positive communication is not just about alleviating Monday blues; it's about creating an environment where employees feel valued, respected, and motivated throughout the week. It requires effort, commitment, and a genuine desire to see others thrive. When executed well, it lays the groundwork for a vibrant, productive, and harmonious workplace, turning the start of the week into an opportunity for growth and positivity.

Providing Incentives and Appreciation

Transitioning from the weekend into a productive workweek doesn't need to feel like an uphill battle against Monday blues. Employers play a pivotal role in shaping this experience, and one of the most impactful strategies they can employ is offering incentives and showing genuine appreciation for their employees. This strategy doesn't just fight against the Monday blues; it transforms them into opportunities for connection, motivation, and enthusiasm for the week ahead.

At the heart of effectively combating Monday blues lies the recognition of employees' efforts. When workers feel valued, their connection to their work deepens, motivating them to start the week with a proactive and positive outlook. The inception of incentives—be it financial bonuses, extra time off, or public acknowledgment—serves as a tangible testament to their value within the company.

Incentive programs tailored to align with employees' needs and interests underscore the employer's commitment to their well-being. For instance, performance bonuses are fantastic, but when companies go the extra mile by offering incentives that support work-life balance, such as flexible scheduling options or opportunities for professional development, they address Monday blues at their core. This holistic approach acknowledges that feeling appreciated extends far beyond the paycheck—it encompasses personal growth and the fulfillment of life outside of work.

Personalized appreciation mechanisms resonate deeply. A simple yet effective strategy is recognizing individual achievements in team meetings or through company communication platforms. Public acknowledgment not only boosts the morale of the recipient but also sets a positive tone for the week, encouraging others to strive for excellence. It's a ripple effect that elevates the entire team's mood and productivity.

Introducing 'Appreciation Mondays' can revitalize the way employees view the start of the week. Imagine walking into work on a Monday to find a personalized thank you note or a small token of appreciation for recent achievements. This kind of initiative fosters a culture of gratitude within the workplace, making Mondays something to look forward to rather than dread.

Yet, incentives and appreciation should not be seen as a one-size-fits-all solution. Flexibility and creativity in their implementation are key. Employers should strive to understand what motivates their individual employees and tailor their approaches accordingly. Surveys and feedback sessions can be invaluable tools for gaining these insights and innovating incentive schemes that truly resonate with the workforce.

Moreover, continuity is critical. Incentives and appreciation should not be isolated events but part of an ongoing effort to create a supportive and motivating work environment. Consistency in recognizing and rewarding effort communicates that every Monday offers a new opportunity to be appreciated and that the company values sustained effort and positivity.

Investments in training and development also serve as incentives, sending a clear message that the company is invested in the employee's future. This approach not only combats Monday blues by providing employees with something to look forward to but also aligns professional growth with personal fulfillment, enriching the overall job satisfaction.

When it comes to battling Monday blues, the element of surprise can also play a significant role. Spontaneous rewards or unexpected gestures of appreciation can inject a burst of positivity into the workplace, breaking the monotony and creating a buzzing atmosphere that carries through the week.

Leadership involvement in incentive and appreciation initiatives is also vital. When leaders actively participate in recognizing employees, it reinforces the culture of appreciation and sets a tone of mutual respect and acknowledgment from the top down. This leadership endorsement can significantly amplify the impact of these initiatives.

It's important to note that while incentives and appreciation are powerful tools, they must be authentic to be effective. Employees can discern between genuine appreciation and token gestures. Therefore, employers should ensure that their actions are sincere and reflective of the company's values and commitment to its workforce.

The battle against Monday blues is multifaceted and requires a proactive approach from employers. By providing thoughtful incentives and showing heartfelt appreciation, companies can turn the tide on Monday blues, creating an environment where employees feel valued, motivated, and eager to start their week. Such a culture not only benefits employees but also enhances overall productivity, fostering a positive and vibrant workplace where every day, especially Monday, holds the promise of recognition, growth, and fulfillment.

Remember, the goal is not just to mitigate the negative aspects of Mondays but to transform them into a launchpad for a successful and satisfying week. By implementing and evolving these strategies, employers can ensure that their workforce not only starts the week off right but also maintains high levels of engagement and satisfaction, paving the way for long-term success and harmony in the workplace.

In navigating the path to a more motivated and appreciated workforce, employers hold the key to turning the dreaded Monday blues into a beacon of positivity and potential. The journey requires commitment, creativity, and a genuine desire to see employees thrive—not just on Mondays, but every day of the week.

Implementing Self-Care Perks

In our exploration of ways to mitigate Monday Blues among employees, one standout strategy is the introduction of self-care perks in the workplace. It's a recognition that well-being goes beyond the physical, into the emotional and mental arenas, where true health flourishes. Companies worldwide are increasingly acknowledging the value of these benefits, identifying them as vital components of a holistic work environment that champions the overall health of their employees.

At the heart of implementing self-care perks is a fundamental shift in how employers view productivity. It's an understanding that an employee who is mentally and emotionally replenished is more focused, engaged, and ultimately, more productive. This chapter delves into practical ways employers can introduce these perks within the workplace, fostering a culture that values and promotes well-being.

Consider the introduction of wellness programs that offer more than just gym memberships. These could include subscriptions to mindfulness apps, on-site meditation sessions, or workshops focusing on mental health. Such initiatives don't just cater to physical health but address stress, anxiety, and depression - contributing factors to the Monday Blues.

Fostering an environment where breaks are encouraged is another critical step. Encouraging employees to take short, frequent breaks during their workday can significantly boost mental agility and combat fatigue. Employers can create designated quiet spaces or relaxation rooms where employees can retreat to recharge.

Flexible scheduling is a self-care perk with substantial impact. Allowing employees to start their day later or providing opportunities to work from home addresses the physical and mental toll of commuting and rigid schedules. This flexibility acknowledges that peak productivity times vary among individuals, fostering a more personalized work environment.

Bringing nature into the office or providing opportunities for employees to reconnect with the outdoors, can also serve as an effective self-care perk. Office designs that incorporate plant life, natural lighting, or even outdoor workspaces contribute to reducing stress and enhancing mood. Similarly, organizing team-building activities outdoors encourages physical activity and team cohesion while providing a break from the office's four walls.

Educational workshops on time management, stress reduction techniques, and nutritional counselling empower employees to take control of their well-being. By providing the tools and knowledge, employers can help staff make informed decisions about their health and lifestyle, ultimately reducing the impact of Monday Blues.

Implementing a 'no meetings day,' specifically on Mondays, can significantly ease the transition into the workweek, allowing employees to plan their work without the interruption of meetings. This can lead to a more productive and less stressful start to their week.

Recognition of personal milestones and providing support during personal challenges can also form part of self-care perks. Celebrating birthdays, work anniversaries, or significant accomplishments fosters a sense of belonging and appreciation, contributing to emotional well-being. Similarly, offering support through counselling services or flexible leave options during challenging times shows a commitment to employees' overall health.

A culture that promotes 'unplugging' after work hours by setting boundaries around email and work communication contributes significantly to mental well-being. Encouraging employees to disconnect allows them time to recharge fully, making them more present and productive during work hours.

Investing in professional development can also be seen as a self-care perk. By supporting employees' career growth and providing opportunities for learning and advancement, employers can boost job satisfaction and engagement, mitigating feelings of stagnation that contribute to Monday Blues.

Offering healthy food options on-site or subsidizing meals can have a positive impact on employees' physical and mental health. Nutrition plays a critical role in mood and energy levels, affecting overall well-being and productivity.

Creating an on-site fitness center or offering fitness classes during work hours not only makes it convenient for employees to prioritize their physical health but also promotes a culture of wellness. This perk addresses the barriers to exercise, such as lack of time or resources, contributing to better health outcomes.

Establishing a feedback mechanism where employees can suggest wellness activities or changes in the workplace ensures that self-care perks remain relevant and beneficial. It demonstrates a commitment to continuous improvement and employee satisfaction.

By embracing these self-care perks, employers can create a work environment where employees feel valued and supported, not just in their professional roles but in their personal well-being. It's a testament to understanding that the health of a company is intrinsically linked to the health of its employees. In doing so, Monday Blues can be transformed from a day of dread to a day of opportunity and growth.

Implementing self-care perks requires a commitment to understanding and investing in the multifaceted well-being of employees. It's about building a workplace that not only drives productivity but also champions the holistic health of every individual. As we venture further into this dialogue, it becomes evident that such initiatives are not just perks but necessary components of a thriving, resilient work culture.

Creating a Supportive Work Environment

In our journey to mitigate Monday blues, one key element stands paramount: creating a supportive work environment. This isn't just about physical space, though that's important. It's about fostering an atmosphere where every employee feels valued, understood, and supported. Here, we delve into how employers can turn their workplaces into havens of support and productivity, addressing one of the most crucial aspects of combating Monday blues.

The first step in this endeavor is to cultivate open communication. This means encouraging employees to speak freely about their concerns, ideas, and feelings without fear of retribution. When people feel heard, they feel valued. Establish regular check-ins and create multiple channels for feedback. This openness not only helps in resolving potential issues before they balloon but also contributes to a sense of community and belonging among staff members.

Next, it's essential to recognize the individuality of each employee. Personalizing support means acknowledging that what works for one might not work for another. Leaders should strive to understand the unique drivers, challenges, and preferences of their team members. This might mean offering different types of workspaces to cater to varied working styles or allowing flexible hours for those who might thrive outside the traditional 9-to-5.

A fundamental cornerstone of a supportive work environment is promoting mental and physical well-being. This can take the form of providing access to wellness programs, mental health days, and ensuring there are quiet, private spaces for relaxation or focused work. Regularly scheduled wellness activities or providing memberships to gyms and meditation apps are excellent ways to show employees that their health is a priority.

Training managers to be more than just supervisors but also mentors is another critical strategy. When managers are equipped to support their team's professional development, employees feel more engaged and valued. This includes having managers who understand the importance of constructive feedback, the power of acknowledgment, and the significance of setting clear, achievable goals.

Encouraging teamwork and fostering a sense of community within the workplace can also significantly impact morale. This doesn't mean forcing team-building exercises that feel more like chores than genuine opportunities for connection. Instead, consider hosting regular social events that are actually fun, encouraging collaborative projects, or setting up interest groups within the company.

In the same vein, creating a culture of recognition and appreciation plays a vital role. Simple gestures, such as a public shoutout for a job well done or a personalized note from a manager, can boost an employee's mood and motivation profoundly. It's about making sure people feel seen and appreciated, not just for their output but for their effort and dedication.

Inclusivity cannot be overlooked if we're to create truly supportive workplaces. This means actively working to dismantle barriers and biases, ensuring equal opportunities for growth and representation at all levels. Celebrating diversity and fostering an environment where everyone, regardless of background, feels welcomed and valued is not just morally right; it's also good business sense.

Providing opportunities for professional advancement is another facet of a supportive work environment. Employees should feel that their workplace is a place of growth, where they can develop their skills, take on new challenges, and advance in their careers. This includes offering training, mentorship programs, and clear pathways for promotion.

A supportive work environment is one that offers safety nets for those times when life gets in the way. This may involve providing paid leave for personal issues, offering support for parents, or even financial advisement services. When employees know they have a cushion to fall back on, they're more likely to feel secure and committed to their job.

The outcome of these efforts is multifaceted. It leads to higher job satisfaction and lower turnover rates, employees who feel supported are more likely to stay with a company long-term, and it fosters higher levels of engagement and productivity. When Monday rolls around, rather than feeling dread, employees who feel supported and valued at work are more likely to feel motivated and optimistic about the week ahead.

Moreover, creating a supportive work environment has a compounding effect. It not only benefits current employees but also helps in attracting top talent. People want to work for companies that care about their employees. In today's world, a company's culture is just as important as the work it does or the compensation it offers.

It's worth noting that creating such an environment requires genuine commitment and effort from the top down. It can't just be a set of policies put down on paper; it needs to be lived and breathed by every member of the organization, from the CEO to the newest intern. It requires a commitment to continuous improvement and openness to change.

A supportive work environment is fundamental in addressing Monday blues and enhancing overall employee wellbeing and productivity. It's about more than just making people feel good—it's about creating a space where everyone can thrive. Through open communication, personalized support, emphasis on health, mentorship, community, recognition, inclusivity, opportunities for growth, and safety nets, employers can create a workplace that not only mitigates the dread of Mondays but also fosters a vibrant, engaged, and committed workforce.

Chapter 7:
Flexibility and Accommodation in the Workplace

In an era where the boundary between work and life is increasingly blurred, the need for flexibility and accommodation at the workplace has never been more critical. The traditional 9-to-5 work schedule, while still prevalent, is starting to feel like a relic of the past for many industries. The demand for a more adaptable approach to work is not just a preference but a necessity for employees striving for a healthier work-life balance. Flexible scheduling allows individuals to tailor their work hours around their personal lives, responsibilities, and peak productivity periods. This chapter delves into how such flexibility can significantly enhance job satisfaction and overall well-being, echoing the broader shift towards a more empathetic and human-centric work culture.

Workplace accommodations go beyond just flexible hours, encompassing a range of modifications and supports designed to meet employees' unique needs. Whether it's ergonomic office furniture to support physical health, technology that aids those with disabilities, or mental health days to support emotional well-being, accommodations are a tangible expression of a company's commitment to its workforce. The impact of these accommodations on employee well-being is profound. They not only increase comfort and reduce stress but also signal to employees that they are valued individuals, not just cogs in a machine. This section will explore the variety of accommodations possible and the positive ripple effects they create across productivity, engagement, and loyalty.

Embracing flexibility and accommodation within the workplace isn't merely about adhering to the latest HR trends—it's about building a future where work serves as a component of a fulfilled life, not a barrier to it. Organizations that recognize and act on this shift stand to benefit from a more motivated, satisfied, and high-performing workforce. By implementing flexible schedules and thoughtful accommodations, employers send a powerful message of respect and empathy towards their employees. This chapter aims to guide employers and employees alike toward understanding the vast benefits of such practices, illustrating that a flexible, accommodating workplace is within reach and mutually beneficial.

Benefits of Flexible Scheduling

The concept of flexible scheduling has emerged as a beacon of hope for many striving to improve their work-life balance and overall job satisfaction. At its core, flexible scheduling empowers individuals to tailor their working hours around personal commitments and preferences, rather than adhering strictly to the traditional nine-to-five routine. This shift can dramatically transform one's experience of Monday mornings, transitioning from dread to anticipation.

Flexible scheduling significantly reduces the stress associated with juggling personal and professional responsibilities. By enabling employees to start and end their day according to personal obligations, such as dropping children at school or attending medical appointments, it cultivates an environment of trust and respect. This autonomy over one's schedule is not just about managing time; it's about recognizing and valuing the individual's whole life outside of work.

Moreover, this scheduling flexibility tends to enhance overall job performance. When individuals have the agency to work during their most productive hours, whether that be early morning or late at night, their output and creativity can soar. We're not all wired the same way; recognizing and accommodating different productivity patterns can lead to remarkable improvements in work quality and efficiency.

Additionally, the option for flexible hours can lead to significant improvements in physical and mental health. The rigid structure of traditional working hours often forces individuals into sedentary lifestyles, with long commutes eating into time that could be spent on exercise or hobbies. Flexible scheduling allows for a more active lifestyle, directly benefiting one's health and, by extension, their productivity and satisfaction with work.

Improved employee retention is another compelling benefit. When employees feel their work-life balance is respected, they're more likely to stay loyal to a company. This is especially pertinent in today's global employment market, where talented individuals have more choice and mobility than ever before.

Flexible scheduling can be a key differentiator for an employer, making it a critical tool for talent retention.

On the topic of talent, flexible scheduling also broadens the talent pool. It opens up employment opportunities to those who might not fit into the traditional work mold, such as parents of young children, students, or those with chronic illnesses. This inclusivity not only enriches the workplace culture but also brings in diverse perspectives that can drive innovation and creativity.

From an economic point of view, companies that adopt flexible scheduling often see a reduction in overhead costs. With more employees working remotely or adhering to staggered schedules, there's less need for large, permanent office spaces. This shift can lead to substantial savings on utilities and office resources, an aspect particularly appealing in the current economic climate.

Environmental benefits also come into play with flexible scheduling. As more people stagger their work hours or work from home, morning and evening commutes become less congested, reducing overall carbon emissions. It's a shift that not only benefits the individual and the company but the planet as a whole.

Employee engagement and motivation are notably higher among those who enjoy flexible schedules. When workers feel trusted to manage their own time, they're more committed to meeting, if not exceeding, expectations. This autonomy fosters a strong sense of ownership and accountability, traits that are invaluable in the modern workplace.

The reduction in absenteeism and tardiness is another tangible benefit. When employees have the flexibility to manage personal issues without sacrificing a day's work, companies see fewer unscheduled absences. This reliability and consistency can significantly impact a team's performance and cohesion.

For companies looking to foster a culture of innovation, flexible scheduling can be a catalyst. By allowing employees to work during their peak creative times, organizations tap into their team's maximum potential. Creativity doesn't thrive in a rigid structure; it needs space and flexibility to flourish.

Flexible scheduling also has a positive impact on company culture. It signals a shift from valuing presenteeism to valuing outcome and performance. This change in mindset helps build a more trusting and respectful company environment, where outcomes are prioritized over mere visibility in the office.

Moreover, this flexibility supports life-long learning and career development. Employees with the freedom to adjust their hours can pursue further education or professional development opportunities, leading to a more skilled and adaptable workforce.

Embracing flexible scheduling can significantly enhance an employer's brand. In an era where prospective employees carefully consider a company's values and culture, flexible work options can make a company more attractive to top-tier talent.

The benefits of flexible scheduling are manifold, impacting every aspect of work-life balance, job performance, and overall satisfaction. For those looking to transform their Monday blues into a more positive start to the week, exploring and advocating for flexible scheduling can be a significant step forward. As we move further into the future of work, it's clear that flexibility and accommodation are not just trends but necessities for fostering happy, productive, and resilient workforces.

The Impact of Workplace Accommodations on Employee Well-Being

When we start to break down the walls of traditional work environments, it's like opening the window on a stuffy afternoon; the fresh air revives us. The concept of workplace accommodations has evolved far beyond physical adjustments or ergonomic chairs. It's a holistic approach that encompasses flexible scheduling, mental health support, and an understanding of diversity and personal needs. These accommodations are not just perks—they're a powerful means to enhance employee well-being.

Consider the employee who's also a caregiver, juggling responsibilities at home and work. The option of a flexible schedule means they can attend to family needs without the constant stress of conflicting obligations. This flexibility isn't just a relief; it's a lifeline that allows for a healthier balance between personal commitments and professional responsibilities.

Then there's the mental health aspect. We're in an era where discussing mental health in the workplace is no longer taboo but encouraged. Accommodations like mental health days, access to counseling, and a supportive culture can make all the difference. Employees who feel supported in their mental health journey are more likely to feel engaged and motivated at work.

These accommodations also speak volumes about a company's culture. They tell employees, "We see you, we hear you, and you matter." This recognition fosters a deep sense of belonging and loyalty. When employees feel valued, their satisfaction and productivity soar, creating a positive feedback loop that benefits everyone.

Adaptability is another cornerstone of workplace accommodations. The traditional 9-to-5 model doesn't fit all lifestyles or productivity patterns. Some people thrive by starting their day earlier, while others do their best work in the evening. Flexibility in work hours accommodates these diverse work styles, allowing employees to work when they're most productive.

Remote work, once considered a temporary solution, has shown tremendous benefits in terms of employee well-being. The lack of commute, the ability to create a personalized workspace, and the flexibility to manage work and home duties concurrently have reduced stress for many. It's a form of accommodation that caters to the modern worker's needs, fostering a better work-life integration.

Onsite accommodations can't be overlooked either. Something as simple as providing a quiet space for breaks or prayer can make employees feel respected and understood. By attending to the varied needs of their workforce, employers build a more inclusive and harmonious workplace.

The feedback from employees who benefit from these accommodations is telling. Many report feeling less stressed, more valued, and more loyal to their employer. This isn't just anecdotal. Research consistently shows that accommodations related to flexibility and mental health support lead to lower absenteeism, higher job satisfaction, and increased productivity.

But it's not all about productivity metrics and bottom lines. It's about people feeling seen and supported, knowing that their employer doesn't just view them as a cog in the machine but as a valuable member of the team. This understanding fosters a stronger emotional connection to their work and their workplace.

Let's not forget that accommodations are a two-way street. Employees who feel supported are more likely to go above and beyond, contributing to a culture of mutual respect and cooperation. This creates a healthier, more dynamic work environment where innovation and creativity flourish.

Employers play a crucial role in this ecosystem. By setting an example and showing a commitment to employee well-being, they pave the way for a more resilient and adaptable workforce. It's a testament to the power of empathy and understanding in transforming the workplace.

In embracing workplace accommodations, we're not just making adjustments for individual needs; we're redefining what a healthy, productive work environment looks like. It's a place where diversity is celebrated, and well-being is prioritized—a space where every employee has the opportunity to thrive.

The impact of workplace accommodations on employee well-being is profound and far-reaching. It's a testament to the notion that when we care for our people, the rewards extend beyond the confines of our office walls. We're not just improving jobs; we're enhancing lives, strengthening communities, and, in many ways, reimagining the future of work.

As we move forward, it's essential to keep the conversation about workplace accommodations alive. It's not a one-time initiative but an ongoing journey towards creating work environments that truly cater to the well-being of every employee. By continuing to listen, adapt, and support, we can ensure that the workplace feels like a place of opportunity and growth for all.

The impact of workplace accommodations on employee well-being cannot be overstated. It's a critical element in the pursuit of a happier, healthier, and more productive workforce. As employers and employees collaborate to foster flexible, supportive, and inclusive work environments, we're not just improving individual lives; we're setting a new standard for what it means to be a part of the modern workforce. And the benefits of this approach? They're as substantial for the organizations as they are for the individuals who propel them forward.

Chapter 8:
Fostering a Culture of
Appreciation and Support

In any workplace, the cultivation of a culture where appreciation and support are woven into the fabric of daily interactions can transform an ordinary job into a source of joy and fulfillment. This chapter dives deep into not just why fostering such a culture is vital but also how it can be achieved. When employees feel valued and supported, their dread for Mondays can diminish, making way for an enthusiasm that permeates through their work and into their work-life balance.

A key element in fostering a culture of appreciation is recognizing the individual efforts of each employee. Acknowledgment doesn't need to be grandiose; sometimes, a simple 'thank you' or 'great job' can enormously impact someone's morale and motivation. Strategies for acknowledging employee efforts might include regular shout-outs during meetings, personalized notes for jobs well done, or a kudos board where peers can post compliments and thanks. This approach not only elevates the mood of individuals but also sets a precedent of positivity and mutual respect within the team.

Creating a positive and supportive work environment goes beyond just recognition. It's about crafting a space where employees feel they can bring their whole selves to work without fear of judgment. This includes open lines of communication, where feedback is not only encouraged but is also given constructively and with empathy. Support should also manifest in the form of resources and tools for personal and professional growth, showing that the organization cares about individual progress as well as collective success.

Moreover, such a culture is not a one-time effort but a continuous process that requires consistent reinforcement. Celebrations of small wins and team milestones should be ingrained practices, fostering a sense of community and shared purpose. Leadership plays a crucial role in this by modeling appreciation and support in their actions and communications, nurturing an environment where these values flourish organically.

Fostering a culture of appreciation and support is not just beneficial but essential for a thriving workplace. It's about creating an ecosystem where Mondays are no longer a source of dread but an opportunity to contribute to a purposeful collective endeavor, enhancing not only job performance but also work-life balance. By implementing the strategies discussed, organizations can make significant strides toward a more positive, supportive, and motivating environment for all employees.

Strategies for Acknowledging Employee Efforts

Embarking on the journey of building a culture that vehemently acknowledges and appreciates the efforts of its workforce is no small feat. It requires a deliberate shift in mindset and the implementation of authentic strategies that resonate with employees at every level. The aim is to pivot from mere transactional interactions to a more heartfelt, recognition-rich environment. This change not only enhances employee morale but also significantly contributes to an individual's sense of belonging and purpose within the organization.

One foundational approach is to personalize recognition. It's crucial to understand that what motivates and matters to one employee might not hold the same value for another. Diving deep into the personal preferences and understanding the unique motivators for each team member can transform a generic acknowledgment into a powerful tool of engagement. Whether it's public recognition for some or a quiet word of genuine thanks for others, the key lies in personalizing the gesture to amplify its impact.

Utilizing technology can also play a pivotal role in acknowledging efforts. In today's digital age, several platforms facilitate real-time recognition and feedback across all levels of an organization. These tools not only make it easier for managers to offer immediate praise but also encourage peer-to-peer recognition, fostering a community of support and encouragement within the workplace. This immediate and often public acknowledgment can significantly elevate an individual's sense of achievement and belonging.

Creating an "Employee of the Month" program can be another effective strategy, offering a regular, formalized method to appreciate outstanding contributions. However, it's essential to ensure these programs are inclusive and equitably distributed across departments and roles. Celebrating achievements across a diverse spectrum of contributions, from stellar client feedback to behind-the-scenes operational improvements, ensures that every effort is valued and recognized.

Implementing a peer-recognition program can democratize the process of acknowledgment. Encouraging employees to recognize their colleagues' contributions can cultivate a positive feedback loop within the team. This peer-to-peer recognition nurtures a supportive atmosphere where appreciation is not solely top-down but is a shared responsibility among all team members.

Offering professional development opportunities as a form of acknowledgment is a profound way to show appreciation. Investing in an employee's growth demonstrates a commitment to their future. This might mean offering courses, workshops, or even roles with more responsibility. It signals trust in their abilities and a desire to see them excel further.

Small tokens of appreciation, though seemingly minor, can make a significant difference. This could range from gift cards to an extra day off, or even a simple thank-you note. These gestures, when tailored to what the employees value, can go a long way in making them feel seen and appreciated.

Incorporating celebration into the workplace culture is vital. This doesn't necessarily mean grand parties, but could include small, consistent acts of celebrating milestones, both professional and personal. Acknowledging birthdays, work anniversaries, or even personal achievements like running a marathon or a family addition, contributes to a warm, inclusive atmosphere.

Transparency in communication also plays a crucial role in acknowledgment. Celebrating team achievements, sharing success stories, and openly discussing challenges not only fosters trust but also ensures that everyone feels valued and an integral part of the company's journey.

Providing flexibility and recognizing the effort it takes to balance work and personal life is also a form of appreciation. By accommodating personal needs through flexible working hours or the option to work remotely, employers can show they value and trust their employees, leading to increased loyalty and job satisfaction.

Feedback loops, when designed constructively, can be a potent acknowledgement tool. Regular, constructive feedback sessions help in recognizing ongoing efforts and discussing areas for growth. This proactive approach ensures that recognition is not just about the outcomes but also about the journey and effort put forth.

Engaging employees in decision-making processes conveys respect and appreciation for their insights and expertise. This inclusivity not only empowers employees but also strengthens their commitment and feel of personal investment in the organization's success.

Creating a culture that celebrates failures as much as successes is vital. Recognizing that setbacks are part of the growth process and appreciating the learnings and resilience they bring can profoundly impact an employee's willingness to innovate and take risks.

Crafting a culture that actively acknowledges and appreciates employee efforts requires a multifaceted approach. It's about creating an environment where everyone feels valued, their contributions are celebrated, and where there is a genuine investment in each individual's growth and well-being. Such a culture not only boosts morale but also drives performance, innovation, and loyalty, ultimately contributing to a more positive and supportive workplace for all.

Creating a Positive and Supportive Work Environment

The journey towards cultivating a workplace that breathes positivity and support might seem daunting at first glance. Yet, it's one of the most rewarding endeavors an organization can embark on. This chapter is dedicated to unraveling how businesses can build an environment where every employee feels valued, supported, and motivated to bring their best self to work.

To start with, understanding what makes a work environment positive and supportive is crucial. It's more than just the physical space or the monetary rewards. It boils down to the culture—the invisible thread that connects every individual within the organization. A culture that celebrates small wins, acknowledges efforts, and provides constructive feedback paves the way for a positive work setting.

Incorporating open communication lines is a foundational step. When employees feel heard and understood, they're more likely to contribute ideas and solutions openly. This doesn't just apply to work-related discussions but extends to personal challenges that might impact an employee's performance. Establishing regular check-ins and feedback sessions can foster this culture of open communication.

Flexibility plays a significant role in demonstrating support for team members. Offering flexible working hours or the option to work remotely shows empathy towards the diverse needs and responsibilities outside of work that employees juggle. This flexibility signals trust and respect, empowering employees to manage their time in a way that optimizes productivity and work-life balance.

Recognition and appreciation are the cornerstones of a supportive work environment. Celebrating milestones, whether they're personal achievements like work anniversaries or professional successes like completing a challenging project, boosts morale and encourages continued excellence. Recognition doesn't always have to be grand gestures; sometimes, a simple 'thank you' or 'well done' can be profoundly impactful.

Team building activities shouldn't be overlooked. They're not just about fun and games but are crucial for building trust and camaraderie among team members. When employees connect on a personal level, collaboration and communication naturally improve, leading to a more harmonious and supportive work environment.

Career development opportunities are also vital. When an organization invests in its employees' growth, it not only benefits the company by enhancing their skills but also shows that the company cares about their career paths. Providing training sessions, mentorship programs, and clear advancement routes can keep employees motivated and engaged.

Health and wellness initiatives reflect an organization's commitment to its employees' overall well-being. This can include offering gym memberships, mental health days, or even just ensuring that the office has ergonomic furniture. Such initiatives help reduce burnout and signal that the company values its employees' health.

Creating a supportive work environment also means fostering inclusivity and diversity. Celebrating differences and ensuring every voice is valued strengthens the organizational culture and encourages a sense of belonging among employees. This includes continuous education on inclusivity and active efforts to eliminate any form of discrimination.

The physical workspace matters too. An environment that's bright, comfortable, and reflective of the company's values can significantly enhance morale and productivity. Whether it's incorporating green spaces or ensuring there are communal areas for employees to relax, the layout and design of the workspace contribute to a positive atmosphere.

Encouraging work-life balance is essential. While hard work is important, understanding that rest and personal time are crucial for rejuvenation is key. Encouraging employees to take their vacation time, not glorifying overtime, and offering support for personal commitments can greatly enhance employee satisfaction and loyalty.

Empowerment through decision-making can also uplift a work environment. Allowing employees to have a say in decisions that affect their work or the workplace gives them a sense of ownership and pride in their contributions. This empowerment helps build a trusting and supportive atmosphere where employees feel their opinions matter.

It's essential to regularly assess the work environment and culture. Gathering feedback from employees through surveys or suggestion boxes can provide valuable insights into how the environment can be improved. Addressing issues promptly and transparently shows that the company is committed to maintaining a positive and supportive work atmosphere.

Creating a positive and supportive work environment is a multifaceted process that requires attention to emotional, physical, and professional needs. It's an ongoing journey that evolves with the organization and its people. By prioritizing these initiatives, companies can foster a culture of appreciation and support, where employees feel valued, motivated, and happy to come to work not just on Mondays, but every day.

As we move on from this section, remember that a positive and supportive work environment is the backbone of a thriving company culture. It's the soil in which the seeds of innovation, collaboration, and excellence are sown and nurtured to fruition. By committing to these principles, organizations can transform the way they work and, ultimately, achieve unparalleled success.

Chapter 9:
Redefining the Meaning of Work

In our journey through life and career, the notion of what work means to us can vastly shift and evolve. This chapter is a deep dive into redefining the essence of work beyond the traditional paycheck, towards a direction where joy, purpose, and satisfaction become the forefront of our daily grind. The quest isn't just to find a job we can tolerate, but to craft a vocation that fills us with passion, invigorates our spirit, and truly matters in the grand scheme of things.

Let's start by acknowledging that finding joy and purpose in your job is more than a luxury; it's a fundamental component of our well-being. Imagine waking up on a Monday morning feeling excited about the day ahead because the work you do aligns with your values and interests. This isn't a far-fetched dream but a possible reality when we start to view our careers through a lens of personal fulfillment and impact, rather than as merely a means to an end.

The importance of meaningful work cannot be overstated. Studies suggest that individuals engaged in work they find meaningful are not only happier but also more productive, resilient, and likely to stay with their employers for longer periods. But how do we navigate this shift towards meaningfulness in our careers? It starts with introspection and a willingness to question and redefine our career goals and aspirations.

Consider the moments in your job that bring you the most joy and satisfaction. It could be the creative problem-solving, the collaboration with a dynamic team, or the knowledge that your work makes a difference in someone's life. These are clues to what meaningful work looks like for you. By focusing on these aspects, you can start to transform even the mundane tasks into parts of a larger, fulfilling mission.

Yet, redefining the meaning of work also involves recognizing its role in our broader lives. Work is not just what we do; it's part of who we are. It's about contributing to something bigger than ourselves, connecting with others, and making use of our talents and abilities. When we start seeing our work as an essential piece of our identity and as a way to express our deepest values, it transforms the notion of a job from a chore into a calling.

Moreover, this shift in perspective opens the door to exploring new opportunities that align more closely with what we find meaningful. It could mean transitioning to a different role within your organization, switching careers, or even starting a new venture. The key is to be open to change and to see these transitions not as risks but as steps towards a more fulfilling professional life.

Of course, redefining your work's meaning isn't always easy. It may require difficult decisions, like leaving a comfortable, well-paying job for something uncertain but more aligned with your passion. It requires courage, resilience, and an unwavering belief in your own capabilities. But the rewards—increased happiness, satisfaction, and a sense of purpose—are undoubtedly worth it.

To support this journey, it's crucial to surround yourself with people who understand and support your quest for meaningful work. Seek out mentors and peers who are on similar paths. Their guidance, advice, and encouragement can be invaluable as you navigate the complexities of aligning your career with your passions.

In the end, redefining the meaning of work is a deeply personal and continuously evolving process. It's about finding balance, seeking joy, and making a difference through our careers. As we progress in this journey, let's remind ourselves that every step taken towards meaningful work is a step towards a more fulfilled life.

Remember, the ultimate goal is not just to improve our Mondays but to transform our entire notion of what it means to work. By redefining the meaning of work, we don't just change how we feel about Mondays; we change our lives.

Finding Joy and Purpose in Your Job

Finding joy and purpose in your job transcends the act of merely showing up to work and going through the motions. It's about redefining your relationship with your work, seeing beyond the tasks and the paychecks into the heart of what you do and why it matters. Discovering joy in your job is akin to uncovering a treasure that's been there all along, hidden beneath layers of routine and expectations.

Many of us spend a significant portion of our lives at work, yet the concept of joy in the workplace often feels elusive. It's easy to fall into the trap of viewing our jobs as something we 'have to do' rather than something we 'get to do.' This mindset shift is fundamental. When you start seeing your job as an opportunity rather than an obligation, the doors to finding deeper satisfaction and purpose swing wide open.

To begin this transformative journey, start by identifying what aspects of your job you genuinely enjoy. It might be the camaraderie with colleagues, the satisfaction of solving complex problems, or the joy of helping others. These are your beacons of light, guiding you toward a more fulfilling work experience. By focusing on these positives, you can begin to cultivate a sense of gratitude for your job.

Gratitude in the workplace is a powerful tool. It transforms your perspective, helping you to see the value in your work and its impact on the larger world. This doesn't mean you should ignore the aspects of your job that are challenging or less enjoyable. Rather, it's about balancing your perspective, acknowledging the good with the bad, and finding ways to make the most out of every situation.

Finding purpose in your job is closely linked to understanding how your work contributes to something larger than yourself. This might mean looking at how your role supports your team, contributes to your company's mission, or impacts the greater good. Knowing that your work has meaning can significantly enhance your job satisfaction and overall happiness.

Another key element in finding joy and purpose in your work is growth. Opportunities for personal and professional development can make your job more engaging and rewarding. Seek out new projects, ask for feedback, and set goals for your career advancement. These actions not only bring variety and challenge into your daily routine but also pave the way for greater fulfillment.

Communication plays a vital role in enhancing job satisfaction. Having open lines of communication with your colleagues and superiors can foster a more positive work environment. It allows you to express your needs and goals, receive support, and build meaningful relationships. Feeling connected and supported at work can significantly boost your sense of belonging and purpose.

The concept of work-life balance is also crucial in finding joy and purpose in your job. While dedicating yourself to your career is important, so too is taking the time to rest and recharge. A well-balanced life ensures that you're bringing your best self to work each day, which in turn, contributes positively to your job performance and satisfaction.

Autonomy in your role can drastically improve how you feel about your job. Having the freedom to make decisions and approach your work in a way that suits you best can lead to increased creativity and innovation. Empower yourself by seeking out projects or tasks that allow for this flexibility and watch how your job satisfaction grows.

The environment you work in can also influence your sense of joy and purpose at work. A positive, encouraging, and aesthetically pleasing workspace can elevate your mood and improve your productivity. Take the time to personalize your space, if possible, and encourage a culture of positivity and collaboration within your team.

Resilience is key to maintaining joy and purpose in your job, especially during challenging times. Learning to adapt to change and face setbacks with a positive attitude can not only make you more valuable to your employer but can also make your work more satisfying. Embrace challenges as opportunities for growth and learning.

It's also important to celebrate successes, no matter how small. Acknowledging and sharing your achievements with your team can foster a sense of accomplishment and pride in your work. These moments of celebration contribute to a positive work culture and remind everyone of the value of their contributions.

Never underestimate the power of helping others. Whether it's mentoring a new employee, collaborating on a project, or simply offering your support, making a positive impact on your colleagues' lives can bring immense joy and satisfaction. It reinforces the idea that your work extends beyond tasks and deadlines – it's about people and relationships.

Finding joy and purpose in your job is an ongoing journey, not a final destination. It requires effort, commitment, and a willingness to see beyond the day-to-day challenges. By embracing this journey, you can transform your work experience, enhance your wellbeing, and perhaps, even change the world in your own small way.

Remember, the quest for joy and purpose in your job is deeply personal and unique. There's no one-size-fits-all approach, but by employing these strategies, you can begin to forge a more meaningful and rewarding career path. Embrace this journey with an open heart and mind, then watch as your relationship with work transforms into something truly fulfilling.

The Importance of Meaningful Work

As we delve deeper into the journey of redefining the meaning of work, it becomes increasingly clear how pivotal meaningful engagement is to our overall happiness and satisfaction. Meaningful work isn't just a buzzword thrown around in the corporate world—it's the essence of a fulfilled life and the antithesis of the dreaded Monday Blues. At its core, meaningful work allows individuals to connect with their deeper values and purposes, significantly elevating not just productivity but also personal contentment and well-being.

The quest for meaning in our professional lives is a testament to the evolving perception of work. No longer are jobs seen merely as a means to an end—today, they're an integral part of our quest for a purpose-driven life. Yet, finding meaning in one's work is no trivial task. It demands introspection, a willingness to challenge the status quo, and often, a leap of faith away from comfort zones. It's about aligning one's career with their core values, passions, and strengths, and in doing so, transforming every Monday from a dreaded day to an opportunity for growth and fulfillment.

But what makes work meaningful? It's a question that might elicit as many responses as there are stars in the sky. For some, it's the pursuit of excellence in a chosen field, while for others, it's the impact their work has on the lives of others. Yet, despite these differences, a common thread unites meaningful endeavors—contribution. Meaningful work contributes to something greater than oneself, offering a sense of purpose beyond the daily grind, and forging connections with others rooted in shared goals and values.

This focus on contribution serves as a powerful antidote to disengagement and dissatisfaction at work. When we see the fruits of our labor contributing to a larger narrative, we're not just motivated; we feel an intrinsic reward that transcends monetary compensation. This isn't to say that financial rewards are unimportant, but rather, that they are part of a broader set of factors that collectively make work truly meaningful.

Meaningful work in a car factory might be the idea of being a part of something such as putting together a portion of a vehicle that helps a family get from here to there safely. Finding meaning at an office cubicle might be the joy of connecting with your cubicle mate or being there for a customer over a phone call. The financial rewards might be the main driving force for some; they work harder to gain incentives so that the financial reward helps them provide for their family, helps them to donate more often to a nonprofit they care deeply about, or the financial reward helps them to achieve life-long travel dreams. Meaning in ones work is truly unique to each individual.

But the path to meaningful work isn't always clear or easy. It's fraught with challenges and uncertainties. One might have to navigate through periods of self-doubt, societal pressures, or even financial constraints. However, it's through facing and overcoming these challenges that one finds clarity and a deeper sense of purpose. It's a journey of discovery, of learning what truly matters to us and how we can make a difference in the world through our work.

Moreover, the pursuit of meaningful work has ramifications beyond the individual. It impacts organizations and societies at large. Employers who recognize and foster environments that allow individuals to find and engage in meaningful work not only boost their productivity and innovation but also contribute to the overall well-being of their workforce. It creates a virtuous cycle where work-life balance is not just an ideal to aspire to but a tangible reality that benefits both the individual and the collective.

In this ever-connected, fast-paced world, the pressure to perform can often lead to burnout and existential despair. However, meaningful work acts as a buffer against these forces. It provides a sense of stability and fulfillment that counteracts the volatility of the modern workplace. This isn't to say that meaningful work is devoid of stress or difficulty, but rather, that these challenges are part of a larger, more rewarding journey.

One of the most transformative aspects of meaningful work is its ability to redefine our relationship with Mondays. Rather than seeing the start of the workweek as a return to drudgery, those engaged in meaningful pursuits view Mondays as a welcome opportunity to continue making a difference. It's a mindset shift that transforms the very fabric of our weekly routines, turning what was once dreaded into something eagerly anticipated.

So, how does one go about finding and fostering meaningful work? It begins with self-reflection. Understanding your own values, passions, and skills is the first step toward aligning your professional path with what truly fulfills you. It's about asking tough questions and being honest with the answers. What do I love doing? What am I good at? How can my work serve others? These are the markers on the road to meaningful work.

But it doesn't stop there. Finding meaningful work is just the beginning; nurturing and sustaining it is an ongoing effort. It requires constant learning, adaptation, and most importantly, resilience. There will be setbacks and failures, but it's through these experiences that we grow and find deeper meaning in our professional journeys.

It's also worth noting that meaningful work is not a luxury afforded only to the few. Regardless of one's profession or position, there is potential for meaningful engagement. From the artist to the accountant, meaning can be found in the pursuit of excellence, the mastery of a craft, or the service of others. It's a universal quest, bound not by profession but by perseverance and passion.

As we move forward in this chapter, we'll explore various pathways to uncovering and cultivating meaningful work. We'll share stories, strategies, and insights to inspire and guide you toward a more fulfilling professional life. It's a journey that promises not just to improve your Mondays, but to transform your entire outlook on work and life.

The importance of meaningful work cannot be overstated. It's a cornerstone of personal fulfillment, job satisfaction, and overall well-being. By finding and engaging in work that resonates with our deeper selves, we unlock the potential to not just endure our professional lives, but to thrive within them. Let this be a call to action—a reminder that life is too short to spend dreading Mondays. Instead, let's embrace the challenge of making every day, especially Monday, a testament to our pursuit of meaning in our work and lives.

Remember, it's not just about making a living; it's about making a life worth living. This pursuit of meaning isn't just a path to personal fulfillment; it's a journey toward creating a world where work enriches, inspires, and connects us all. Let's redefine the meaning of work together, one Monday at a time.

Conclusion

As we reach the end of our journey together, it's vital to reflect on the ground we've covered and the changes we've envisioned for our lives, especially when it comes to transforming our Mondays and improving our work-life balance and job performance. The steps outlined in the preceding chapters are not mere suggestions; they are pillars upon which we can build a more fulfilling life, both personally and professionally.

Understanding the Monday Blues is the first step towards overcoming them. Recognizing that these feelings are not just in our heads but have tangible causes and effects gives us the power to address them. We've delved deep into the roots of these blues, examining various factors from job dissatisfaction to physical health, and armed ourselves with the knowledge to combat them.

Improving our work-life balance is no small feat, but the strategies shared have been designed to gently guide us towards a more harmonious existence. Whether it's by optimizing our schedules or fostering positive relationships at work, each chapter has laid out practical steps to make each day, not just Mondays, significantly better.

Enhancing job performance goes hand in hand with boosting our overall happiness and well-being. By finding joy in what we do, seeking continuous improvement, and maintaining motivation beyond Monday, we've discovered that our professional success is a byproduct of a well-balanced, fulfilling life.

The role of employers in this journey cannot be understated. Creating an environment that values work/life balance, flexibility, and employee well-being is critical. We've seen how adopting these practices not only benefits employees but also contributes to the overall success and sustainability of the organization.

Let's not forget the importance of flexibility and accommodation in the workplace. By embracing these values, we open the door to a more inclusive and supportive work environment, which in turn can lead to increased job satisfaction and reduced stress for everyone involved.

Fostering a culture of appreciation and support plays a crucial role in our quest for a happier work-life. When we feel valued and recognized for our efforts, it fuels our motivation and commitment, making even the most challenging Mondays easier to face.

Redefining the meaning of work is perhaps the most profound step we can take. By finding purpose and joy in our jobs, we transform them from mere sources of income into integral parts of our quest for a fulfilling life. This shift in perspective is essential for overcoming the Monday Blues and embracing each day with enthusiasm and positivity.

However, it's important to remember that progress is a journey, not a destination. The strategies and insights shared in this book are not one-time fixes but tools to be used continuously throughout our careers and lives. It's about making small, consistent changes that add up to a big difference in how we feel about Mondays and work in general.

Embracing flexibility in our approach is also key. What works for one person might not work for another, and our needs and circumstances can change over time. Thus, staying open to adjusting our strategies and habits is crucial for long-term success.

Let's also emphasize the importance of self-care in this equation. While it's easy to get caught up in the hustle of improving job performance and fostering work-life balance, taking time for ourselves—be it through hobbies, relaxation, or simply doing nothing—is vital. Self-care is not selfish; it's a necessary component of our overall well-being and effectiveness.

Remembering your purpose and doing something you love can light up even the darkest Monday mornings. If we find meaning and satisfaction in our work, we're not only more likely to excel but also to feel happier and more content in every aspect of our lives.

Finally, rethinking our jobs and their role in our lives can sometimes mean making bold changes, whether seeking a new position, changing career paths, or even starting our own venture. Such decisions should be made with careful consideration, empowered by the understanding and strategies we've gained.

In closing, the journey to improving our Mondays, work-life balance, and job performance is ongoing and ever-evolving. By embracing the principles and strategies discussed, we equip ourselves with the tools needed not just to face Mondays but to look forward to them with optimism and enthusiasm. Here's to brighter Mondays and a more fulfilling work-life ahead.

Remember, it's within our power to change our lives, one Monday at a time.

Appendix A:
Appendix

Welcome to the Appendix! If you're seeking to dive deeper into enhancing your Mondays, fine-tuning your work-life balance, and elevating your job performance, you've landed in the right spot. This section is a treasure trove of supplementary resources and practical exercises, designed to complement the strategies and insights shared throughout the book. Whether you're looking to manage stress more effectively or infuse your mindset with positivity, the tools you'll find here can serve as stepping stones to a more fulfilling workweek.

Additional Resources for Improving Work-Life Balance and Overcoming Monday Blues

As we navigate through the myriad ways to enhance our work-life balance and push back against the Monday blues, it becomes evident that a plethora of resources are available at our fingertips. Tapping into these can significantly improve the struggles we encounter at the start of our workweek and lead to a more fulfilling career and personal life.

Books are a tremendous source of knowledge and inspiration, offering insights into the experiences of others who've successfully overcome challenges similar to our own. Titles focusing on time management, personal development, and mindfulness are particularly relevant. They can provide strategies for prioritizing tasks, setting achievable goals, and living in the moment—all of which are crucial for maintaining a healthy balance between work and leisure. Explore titles focused on productivity, happiness, and mindfulness. These readings can offer new perspectives and practical tips for crafting a more balanced life.

Numerous **online platforms** provide a wealth of articles, downloadable tools, and interactive communities. Engage with content that speaks to overcoming challenges and celebrating victories, big and small.

Podcasts, too, have surged in popularity as a means of gathering information and advice while on the go. Many podcasts are dedicated to discussing work-life balance, productivity, and happiness, featuring experts from various fields. These can be an excellent way to gain new perspectives and learn practical tips for making the most of your Mondays and the rest of the week. Integrating podcasts into your routine can be a great way to gain insights while on the go. Listen to episodes from thought leaders and practitioners for motivation and strategies that resonate with your personal and professional goals.

Workshops and seminars offer interactive opportunities to delve deeper into the subjects of work-life balance and overcoming negativity. Engaging directly with thought leaders and peers can provide a sense of community and shared purpose, making it easier to adopt new habits and mindsets.

Online forums and social media groups focusing on personal development and professional growth can also be invaluable. Here, members share their experiences, challenges, and successes, providing both support and accountability to one another. This sense of belonging can significantly boost your motivation and resilience.

Exercise has been shown to reduce stress and improve overall mood, making it a powerful tool for combating the Monday blues. Finding an activity you enjoy, whether it's yoga, running, or cycling, and incorporating it into your weekly routine can make a noticeable difference in your physical and emotional well-being.

Nutrition plays a key role in how we feel both physically and mentally. Resources on healthy eating, such as blogs, cookbooks, and nutritional planning tools, can help you make better food choices that boost your energy and mood.

Mindfulness and meditation apps are designed to help users cultivate a habit of present-moment awareness, which can reduce stress and anxiety. Regularly using these apps can help create a more peaceful mind, better equipped to deal with the challenges of work and life.

Time management tools and apps can help you more effectively plan your day, ensuring that you're allocating enough time for both work and relaxation. Learning to prioritize tasks and eliminate unnecessary activities can free up more time for what truly matters.

Professional counseling services, whether in-person or online, can offer personalized guidance and support for dealing with work-related stress, anxiety, and depression. Sometimes, having a professional listen to your concerns and provide strategies for coping and improving your situation can make all the difference.

Career coaching is another resource for those feeling stuck or dissatisfied in their current jobs. A career coach can offer advice on making a change, whether it's moving up in your current field or switching to a new one entirely.

For those interested in **further education**, evening or online courses can provide new skills and qualifications that open up career advancement opportunities. Furthermore, engaging in lifelong learning can be incredibly fulfilling, providing a sense of achievement and purpose.

Volunteering offers a way to give back to your community while gaining a broader perspective on life and work. It can be a source of immense satisfaction and a great way to meet people with similar interests and values. This can indirectly improve your attitude towards work and life.

Adopting a **hobby or interest** that you're passionate about can provide a much-needed escape from work pressures, giving you something to look forward to outside of the office. Whether it's painting, playing an instrument, or gardening, hobbies can enhance your creativity, reduce stress, and improve your mood.

As we've seen, a wealth of resources exists to help us improve our work-life balance and conquer the Monday blues. Engaging with these resources, whether through reading, listening, learning, or doing, can provide the tools and motivation needed to make positive changes. It's about finding what works for you and incorporating it into your weekly routine. With the right approach, overcoming the Monday blues isn't just possible—it's within reach.

Practical Exercises for Stress Management and Positive Thinking

As we close this comprehensive guide on improving Mondays, enhancing work-life balance, and boosting job performance, let's focus on actionable strategies. The journey towards a more fulfilling work life is paved with personal effort and mindful practices. In this section, we provide you with a toolkit of practical exercises dedicated to managing stress and fostering positive thinking. Embracing these techniques can significantly transform not just your Mondays, but every day of your workweek.

Managing stress and maintaining a positive outlook are crucial for overcoming the Monday blues and achieving work-life harmony. The following exercises are designed to build resilience, foster positivity, and enhance your overall well-being:

1. **Gratitude Journaling:** At the end of each day, jot down three things you're grateful for. This simple practice can shift your focus from what's lacking to appreciating what's abundant in your life.

2. **Mindful Breathing:** Whenever you feel overwhelmed, take a moment for some deep, mindful breathing. Inhale for a count of four, hold for four, and exhale for four. This can help calm the mind and center your thoughts.

3. **Positive Affirmations:** Start your morning by affirming your worth and capabilities. Choose affirmations that resonate with you and repeat them daily to build confidence and positivity.

When you find yourself overwhelmed, a simple yet effective strategy is to pause and focus on **deep, slow breathing**. Inhale for a count of four, hold that breath for a count of four, and then exhale slowly for a count of eight. This method, known as the 4-7-8 technique, can swiftly bring calmness, reducing immediate stress and redirecting your focus to the present moment.

Positive visualization is another powerful tool at your disposal. Begin each day, especially Mondays, with a five-minute visualization exercise. Picture your day unfolding in the most positive way possible. Imagine yourself handling challenges with grace, completing tasks with efficiency, and ending the day feeling accomplished. This mental practice sets a hopeful tone for the day and enhances your resilience against potential stressors.

Journaling offers a dual benefit for stress management and cultivating positive thinking. Each evening, dedicate a few minutes to jot down three things that went well that day and what role you played in these positive experiences. This exercise, rooted in positive psychology, encourages you to shift focus from problems and frustrations to achievements and happiness, gradually rewiring your brain to be more optimistic.

Incorporating **affirmations** into your daily routine can also profoundly impact your mindset. Create a list of positive, empowering statements that resonate with you and your goals. Phrases like "I am capable of overcoming any challenge" or "I bring value to my team" can be powerful motivators. Repeat these affirmations during your morning routine to set a positive tone for the day.

Exercise is a well-known stress reliever that also boosts positive thinking. A simple daily walk, a yoga session, or a quick workout can release endorphins, combat stress, and elevate your mood. Try to integrate physical activity into your daily routine, even if it's just a 10-minute burst of movement, to experience its beneficial effects on both your body and mind.

Next, explore **muscle relaxation** techniques to combat physical manifestations of stress. Progressive muscle relaxation involves tensing each muscle group for a few seconds and then releasing it, which can be particularly effective before sleep. This practice not only aids in relieving tension but also promotes a greater sense of calm throughout the body and mind.

Listening to music or podcasts that inspire or relax you can also play a crucial role in managing stress and fostering positivity. Whether it's during your commute, on a break, or while completing tasks, the right audio content can lift your spirits, provide valuable insights, and even offer a sense of connection.

Don't overlook the power of **scheduling something fun or rewarding** for yourself, especially on Mondays. Having something to look forward to can significantly lessen the dread of starting the workweek and increase your overall happiness. Whether it's a special coffee, a lunch date, a movie night, or time dedicated to a hobby, this practice gives you a boost of positivity and motivation.

Maintaining work-life balance is essential for long-term stress management and positive thinking. Firmly delineate your work hours and personal time. Make a conscious effort to unplug from work-related communications after hours to rejuvenate fully. This clear boundary helps reduce burnout and ensures that personal time truly contributes to your well-being.

Remembering your purpose and doing something you love is crucial for positive thinking. Aligning daily tasks with your larger goals can transform mundane activities into meaningful pursuits. If there's a discrepancy between your job and your passions, consider how you can bring more of what you love into your work or how you can pivot towards a role that better fits your aspirations.

To rethink your job in a positive light, regularly identify aspects of your work that you're grateful for. **Gratitude** can significantly alter your perception, turning obstacles into opportunities and transforming challenges into valuable experiences. Regular reflection on the positive aspects of your job can also enhance job satisfaction and fulfillment.

Engaging in community or team activities at work can foster a positive mindset and reduce stress. Building strong relationships with colleagues can provide a supportive network, enhance your sense of belonging, and create a more positive work environment. Try to engage in or initiate team-building exercises or community outreach programs through your workplace.

Finally, it's essential to **seek continuous improvement**, both personally and professionally. Embrace challenges as opportunities for growth and learn from every experience. This mindset not only reduces stress caused by fear of failure but also propels you towards a more positive and fulfilling career path.

Remember, the journey to improving your Mondays, enhancing your work-life balance, and boosting your job performance is ongoing. It's about making small adjustments, celebrating progress, and being kind to yourself along the way. Use the resources and exercises provided as companions on your path to a more satisfying and balanced life. By incorporating these practical exercises into your daily routine, you'll equip yourself with the tools needed to manage stress effectively and cultivate a positive mindset. Transforming your Mondays, and indeed every workday, into more enjoyable and productive experiences is not only possible but within your reach. Let these strategies guide you towards greater work-life harmony, enhanced job performance, and an overall happier life.